Awatif Ata Elmannan Elageed

Weaving the Social Networks of Women Migrants in Sudan

Awatif Ata Elmannan Elageed

Weaving the Social Networks of Women Migrants in Sudan

The Case of Gezira

LIT

Umschlagbild: Grafik von Awatif Ata Elmannan Elageed

Gedruckt mit der Unterstützung
des Evangelischen Entwicklungsdienstes (EED)

Dissertation zur Erlangung des akademischen Grades doctor rerum agriculturarum (Dr. rer. agr.), eingereicht an der Landwirtschaftlich-Gärtnerischen Fakultät der Humboldt-Universität zu Berlin

Bibliographic information published by the Deutsche Nationalbibliothek
The Deutsche Nationalbibliothek lists this publication in the Deutsche Nationalbibliografie; detailed bibliographic data are available in the Internet at http://dnb.d-nb.de.

ISBN 978-3-8258-1726-8
Zugl.: Berlin, Humboldt-Universität, Diss., 2007

A catalogue record for this book is available from the British Library

Verlagskontakt:
Fresnostr. 2 D-48159 Münster
Tel. +49 (0) 2 51/620 32 - 22 Fax +49 (0) 2 51/922 60 99
e-Mail: lit@lit-verlag.de http://www.lit-verlag.de

Auslieferung:
Deutschland/Schweiz: LIT Verlag Fresnostr. 2, D-48159 Münster
Tel. +49 (0) 2 51/620 32 - 22, Fax +49 (0) 2 51/922 60 99, e-Mail: vertrieb@lit-verlag.de
Österreich: Medienlogistik Pichler-ÖBZ GmbH & Co KG
IZ-NÖ, Süd, Straße 1, Objekt 34, A-2355 Wiener Neudorf
Tel. +43 (0) 2236/63 535-290, +43 (0) 2236/63 535 - 243, mlo@medien-logistik.at

Distributed in the UK by: Global Book Marketing, 99B Wallis Rd, London, E9 5LN
Phone: +44 (0) 20 8533 5800 – Fax: +44 (0) 1600 775 663
http://www.centralbooks.co.uk/html

Distributed in North America by:

Transaction Publishers
New Brunswick (U.S.A.) and London (U.K.)

Transaction Publishers
Rutgers University
35 Berrue Circle
Piscataway, NJ 08854

Phone: +1 (732) 445 - 2280
Fax: + 1 (732) 445 - 3138
for orders (U. S. only):
toll free (888) 999 - 6778
e-mail:
orders@transactionspub.com

Dedication

With a very deep sense of humility, I dedicate this work first to my late, most loving father, Ata Elmannan Elageed whose wish for me has been fulfilled by the completion of this work.

To my dearest mother, Rugaia El-Tahir Hamdalla who taught me the meaning of education and sacrificed the pleasures of life to invest time and effort in us. For your exemplary love and affection I am profoundly indebted.

To my beloved, most caring and understanding husband, Musa Mohamed Musa. For your inestimable love, encouragement and lavish care showered on me, I sincerely dedicate my effort.

To the memory of my dearest late aunt Fatma Mohamed Dafa-Allah (Bit El-Shaweesh). It is extremely painful that fate did not allow you to witness the completion of this work, yet it is consoling that we could reach this distance.

To the two women and two men in my life I hereby forward
my deepest appreciation, love and respect.
To you four I dedicate my effort

Preface

The Gezira Scheme ist one of the largest irrigations systems of the world. Dating back to 1926, when under British colonial rule the production of cotton was given much promotion, and after independence 1956 continued and expanded under the Sudanese administration, the scheme over the years saw major changes and numerous ups and downs. In particular, it saw the substantial influx of migrants of different origins.

In the meantime an important body of research, publications, agency reports on various technical and social aspects of the Gezira Scheme exists. Most of it is written in an interventionist perspective, to manipulate technical features, improve economic opportunities and social conditions, adjust management arrangements and the like.

This book takes an entirely different approach. It explores concepts and notions that guide research and the perception of social reality. In so doing it focuses specifically on what has barely been broached in the literature on the Gezira Scheme, the female migrant community. It looks at the social interaction between women migrants of different regions and generations, the social networks they form as well as function and functioning of these networks.. This in turn has repercussions for the concepts underlying social network and actor-oriented theory and methodology. These tend to present themselves in gender neutral terms, by implication ignoring the gender dimension of social interaction and networks and the specificities of gendered dynamics operating in them.
Thus the book performs an, as it were, double loop. In combining social network theory with an actor-oriented approach, both framed in constructivist terms, it throws light on the minutae of the interaction and networking of female migrant workers. By the same token a discussion of conventional concepts reveals the need to introduce additional notions in order to actually capture the rich texture of gender-differentiated and gendered social realities.

The women we are getting to know here are actors in their own right. They defy superficial assumptions of submission and passive acceptance of social gender attributions. While settling in their new work environment they actively seek to access and to build social networks, they engage in interaction and, in the process, find creative compromises concerning ethnicicity-based differences of culture and creed. In the study women are portrayed as architects of their lives, they make decisions, they exercise agency. It could be argued that the gendered social frames and the limits to such agency are down-played in this scenario. But it does go a long way in pointing to the limits of conventional social network theory and in enriching it.

As we learn about the structures of women's work in the Gezira Scheme, the forms of mutual help and collectivity, the interplay with the domestic sphere and with efforts to obtain some measure of social security, about factors making for cohesion or lack thereof, an entire landscape unfolds in front of our eyes. It is a landscape dense with interaction structures and shaped by social categories such as ethnicity, clan, age, formative years, expectations in life, tradition, property rights, division of labour and, in and through all of this, gender orders. It is in this landscape that women weave their networks. The networks serve multiple purposes ranging from securing an income, managing domestic chores, and coping with bottlenecks and times of distress. And they are by no means static. Socio-economic change is having an impact as has the constant re-interpreation of the meaning of gender in processes of personal growth. We also learn that, contrary to superficial depictions, women's networks are by no means homogenious. The study retraces in great detail the numerous factors which make for highly differentiated sub-structures which at times require strategies of containment but can also be made us of.

On the level of theory construction we learn about the need to broaden and to differentiate given concepts, to add and to develop new ones. Both levels are closely related and, rightfully so, constantly intertwined – which makes for fascinating and challenging reading.

Professor Dr. Claudia von Braunmühl
Hon. Professor of Political Science
Free University of Berlin
Germany

Acknowledgements

I am so grateful to the women migrants in the Gezira Scheme who accepted me whole – heartedly into their everyday life and enabled me to forge links and to weave into their social networks. I would like to sincerely thank my first supervisor, Professor Dr. Friedhelm Streiffeler of Humboldt University of Berlin for his encouragement and support since the time of choice of the topic and who gave my involvement in this area an academic direction. I am so grateful for his supervision, constructive comments and for providing me with related literature from his own library.

I am highly indebted to my second supervisor Professor Dr. Claudia von Braunmühl of the Free University of Berlin for her steady guidance, intellectual advice, constructive debates, insightful suggestions, and careful reading throughout all stages of the study. My special thanks are also due to Dr. Parto Teherani-Krönner of Humboldt University of Berlin for her valuable criticism, unstinting support and encouragement throughout the course of the study.

I am also grateful to many individuals particularly to Professor Dr. Günter Lorenzl of Humboldt University of Berlin and Dr. Ulrike Schultz of the Free University of Berlin for all means of support they rendered at the early stages of the study. I wish to thank Professor Dr. Ute Luig of the Free University of Berlin for formulating my ideas at the early stages of writing the proposal. I am also thankful to Dr. Rozaline Achieng from Kenya for her valuable comments on the theoretical approach of the study.

I owe a great deal to the 'Evangelischer Entwicklungsdienst' (EED) for its generous financial assistance which made it possible for me to study in Germany. I am profoundly indebted to Dr. Rudolf Ficker, the head of the EED-scholarship desk for his concern and support. I will never forget Mrs. Susanne Werner, the Academic Advisor of the EED-scholarship desk who remains a constant source of encouragement and whose tirelessly support and valuable advices through out the course of my study in Berlin was very supportive.

I am thankful to Professor Dr. Gasim Badri, the president of Ahfad University for Women (AUW), Omdurman, Sudan, for releasing me to study in Germany. I am immensely grateful to Professor Dr. Balghis Badri of the Institute of

Women, Gender and Development Studies, AUW, Sudan; her concern and untiring support from a distance is unforgettable.
I would also like to extend my thanks to my colleague Ismail Moumouni of Benin for sharing his intellectual experiences with me and for his collegial company.

My time in the Gezira area during the fieldwork was greatly enriched by those who welcomed me into their homes. The family of my late uncle Hamdallah M. Hamdallah, particularly my beloved cousin Sanaa Hamdalla, the family of Mahgoub M. Gaafar, particularly Noor Yousif Elbushra and her beloved daughters Omaima and Lamya, I shall always be grateful for their generosity and support.

My thanks also goes to Mrs. Frauke Pietsch of the 'Korrektur-Büro' in Dublin and Mr. Giles Schumm who edited the manuscript.

It would be impossible to name all those who contributed one way or another during this study and to whom I am profoundly grateful.

Last but not least, I express my heart-felt thanks and love to my family in Khartoum North and Kosti and to all my friends in Sudan and Europe.

Table of contents

List of figures

List of appendices

Summary

Social networks analysis, theories and concepts have not featured in discussion and analysis of the Gezira Scheme, neither officially nor unofficially, and certainly not with attention to gender. Therefore, this study addresses the question of social networks of women migrants in Sudan, taking women migrants in the Gezira Scheme as a central analytical group. The large scale agricultural, irrigated Gezira Scheme is considered a melting pot for women migrants belonging to various African ethnic groups, due to internal and external migration.

The social networks of women migrants are based on partial networks. Theoretical notions of social network analysis and applications that motivate the analysis and interpretation of the empirical data are used. The analysis is also based on an actor-oriented approach developed by Norman Long (1992, 2001).

The empirical research, as with the analysis, is based on qualitative research methods. The analysis is mainly based on empirical data collected in six months in two localities in the Gezira Scheme, where a locality comprises a village of the local community and the surrounding camps of the migrants. The empirical research was conducted using semi-structured interviews, group discussions and observations.

Examining the social networks of women migrants in the Gezira Scheme provides new important insights on social networks theory and additions to the actor-oriented perspective.

Unlike the trauma associated with many cases in which women are considered as subordinated, vulnerable or excluded, this study provides evidence that women are not passive recipients but, on the contrary, social actors in their societies. That women acquire agency and are social actors is evident in the way women benefit from the construction of their social networks and their ability to take advantage of the given circumstances, a significant finding which is considered by this study to be an addition to Long's actor-oriented perspective. However, the study does not just postulate additions to the actor-oriented perspective but it also proposes new contribution.

‘Transitivity’ has been shown to be a key property in women’s social networks as well as a common feature explaining women migrants’ social structure. The analysis shows how ‘transitivity’ is not only associated with ‘clusterability’ as such, as it is known in the social networks theory, but also in the consideration of the concepts of ethnicity and gender - a new contribution to social network theory and analysis by this study.

Zusammenfassung

In Diskussionen und wissenschaftlichen Untersuchungen über das Gezira-Projekt („Gezira Scheme“) wurden bisher Theorien, Ansätze und Konzepte zu sozialen Netzwerken nicht berücksichtigt. Auch hat eine Untersuchung der Gender-Aspekte keine Aufmerksamkeit erlangt. Somit beschäftigt sich diese Studie mit dem Thema soziale Netzwerke von Migrantinnen im Sudan, wobei die Migrantinnen des Gezira-Projekts die zentrale analytische Gruppe sind. Betrachtet wird das groß angelegte ackerbauliche und bewässerungstechnische Gezira-Projekt: ein Schmelztiegel für Migrantinnen, die infolge interner und externer Migration zu verschiedenen ethnischen Gruppen Afrikas gehören.

Die sozialen Netzwerke von Migrantinnen beruhen auf Teilnetzwerken. Es werden theoretische Ansätze von sozialen Netzwerksanalysen und deren Anwendungsmöglichkeiten hinzugezogen, un die Analyse und Interpretation der vor Ort ermittelten empirischen Daten durchzuführen. Außerdem basiert die Untersuchung auf einer Akteur-orientierten Herangehensweise, welche von Norman Long (1992, 2001) entwickelt wurde.

Die empirischen Erhebungen als auch die Analyse beruhen auf qualitativen Untersuchungsmethoden. Die empirischen Daten wurden im Zeitraum von sechs Monaten in zwei Orten des Gezira-Projektes gesammelt, wobeiein Untersuchungsgebiet ein Dorf der örtlichen Kommune und umliegende Migranntenlager umfasst. Die empirische Forschung wurde mittels halbstrukturierter Interviews, Gruppendiskussionen und teilnehmender Beobachtungen durchgeführt.

Die vorliegende Untersuchung von sozialen Netzwerken von Migrantinnen im Gezira-Projekt liefert neue wichtige Einblicke in die Theorie sozialer Netzwerke und Ergänzungen zur Akteur-orientierten Perspektive.

Im Unterschied zum dem Trauma, wonach Frauen als untergeordnet, verletzlich oder ausgeschlossen betrachtet werden, liefert diese Studie einen Beweis dafür, dass Frauen keine passiven Rezipienten sind, sondern im Gegenteil als soziale Akteure in ihren Gesellschaften agieren. Dass Frauen Ämter akquirieren und als soziale Akteure handeln, wird darin deutlich, wie sie von ihren sozialen Netzwerkskonstruktionen und ihrer Fähigkeiten sich die gegebenen Umstände zu

Nutze zu machen, profitieren. Dieses signifikante Ergebnis wird in der Studie als eine Ergänzung zu Long`s Akteur-orientierter Perspektive vorgestellt. Die Studie bezieht sich nicht nur ergänzend auf die Akteur-orientierter Perspektive, sonderen sie bittet auch einen neuen Beitrag.

Es wurde gezeigt, dass „Transitivität" sowohl eine Schlüsseleigenschaft in den sozialen Netzwerken von Frauen ist, als auch eine Gemeinsamkeit, welche die soziale Struktur von Migranntinnenverbänden erklärt. Die Analyse zeigt, dass „Transitivität" nicht nur mit Gruppenfähigkeiten („clusterability") verbunden ist, so wie es aus der Theorie sozialer Netzwerke bekannt ist, sondern ein neuer Beitrag dieser Studie führt zu Überlegungen von Ethnizitäts- und Genderkonzepten: darin liegt der neue Beitrag zur Netzwerktheorie und –analyse.

1. Social networks of women migrants in Sudan

"The science of social networks is the science of the real world – the world of people." **(Watts 2003: 13)**

1.1 Aims and rationale

In recent decades, the social and behavioural science community has expressed considerably increased interest in the analysis of social networks. However, in the case of the Sudan Gezira Scheme (SGS), social networks analysis, theories and concepts have not yet featured in discussion and analysis of the Scheme, neither officially nor unofficially and certainly not with attention to gender. As a result, despite the great number of women migrants in the Gezira Scheme and their substantial role in the agricultural work, no research has been done on their social networks. Instead, the existing studies have limited their definition and analysis of labour and work relations to the domain of economics. Almost all of them tend to neglect the social dynamics and the local processes of social relations and structures. This is because the issue they have chosen to examine does not serve in highlighting social ties and social relations and structures based on social, traditional and cultural incidences, or because most economists focus on quantified relationships. Therefore, they have not looked at the conditioning role of local social and cultural processes. Moreover, the gender dimension has been totally omitted. Hence, this study contends that, apart from the three partnership based production relations between the Government of the Sudan, the Sudan Gezira Board (SGB) and the tenants, other forms and varieties of social relations exist among the Gezira Scheme communities and influence or govern their labour. Instead of limiting the analysis to the production relations between the three partners (The Sudan Government, The Sudan Gezira Board and the tenants) in the Gezira Scheme, this study fundamentally addresses the issue of social networks. It aims at analysing forms and varieties and formalisations of social networks existing among the Gezira Scheme communities, focussing on the women migrants engaged in the agricultural labour force.

The study argues that the underlying assumption reported in literature by sociologists such as Menjivar (1995), which states that networks always provide a haven of support for immigrants, has been left unquestioned in the Sudan Gezira Scheme. Thus, this study looks at the social interactions, social actions and social processes that shape the everyday life of these women as migrants within the Gezira Scheme social context. It examines how women migrants cope in entering and experiencing the working atmosphere in the Gezira scheme. The study also explores how these women cope with their everyday life struggles within their own communities.

This study also argues that women migrants' experiences of their everyday life and construction of their social networks are largely determined by the following complex situation: The relocation of these women migrants transports the cultural background of their societies of origin to the new social world of the Gezira Scheme and engages them in a new kind of economic activity bearing little relation to the traditional subsistence agriculture in their place of origin. In addition to that, the study contends that women construct their social life through a diversity of social interactions and social actions within their own communities. This becomes more interesting when one sees that most of these women are originally of non-Sudanese ethnic backgrounds within the Sudan social context. Menjivar (1995) supports this view; social networks are undoubtedly shaped by the interplay of specific characteristics of the group in question and broader forces in the receiving context (Menjivar 1995: 220). The social system of the migrant communities consists of a set of work relations, gender relations and highly traditional networks of relations such as ethnic and neighbourhood relations. Understanding these networks with a focus on women migrants is essential in comprehending the nature of these women's lives in the Gezira Scheme (ref. to: Rogers 1881: 89).

It is important to report at the outset of this study that the migrants in the Gezira Scheme are settled in camps surrounding the villages of the local community. This system of settlement was a policy set by the British colonial rule in Sudan (1898–1956) which established the Gezira Scheme in 1925/26. Moreover, the Sudanese governments, post independence, have followed the British in settling the migrants in camps. Grätz, a German social anthropologist argues that social and ethnic heterogenisation could be a reaction to different forms of State intervention (Grätz, 2000: 4). This study argues that the question of social and ethnic heterogeneity is also largely based on how these communities classify themselves and how they are socially interrelated. Quoting Grätz: *"Stable social relations, ties of affection and common basic ethical assumptions are generally elements which generate trust, stabilise social networks and guarantee economic stability, especially outside formally-legal regulations"* (ibid: 16).

The general debate in this study focuses on how women migrants interact by means of their social networks within the broader migrants and local communities in the Gezira Scheme. It examines how women migrants socially interact in their everyday life, how they cooperate and how they work collectively to support each other.

In light of the above, this study offers an empirical analysis of social networks in present day Sudan, taking the case of women migrants in the Gezira Scheme as a central analytical group. The aim of this study is to depict women migrants' social networks by looking into social networks formalizations and their importance at various levels. These encompass women's daily social interactions and experiences and the problem-solving strategies they apply within the work sphere as well as within their private sphere. As to the structural level, the study looks into gender order and gender relations. Gender is considered by this study as a relational concept as gender requires two sets of gender identities, usually women and men (Schmidt 2000:2). Hence, gender relations refer to the ways in which the social categories of women and men relate to one another over the range of social organisation (Purewel 1998: 1–3). Gender relations as a form of social relations can be defined, as Kabeer (1992) postulates, as dimensions of social relations which create, underline and reinforce systematic differences in the positioning of women and men in social processes (Kabeer 1992: 17).

1.2 Analytical focus of the study

Examining the social networks of women migrants, theoretical notions of social network analysis and applications that motivate a qualitative analysis and interpretation of the empirical data are used. The analysis is also based on an actor-oriented perspective developed by Norman Long (1992, 2001). The conceptual foundation of an actor-oriented analysis brings together specific key elements; that social life is heterogeneous or polymorphic. That it is comprised of a wide diversity of social forms and cultural repertoires, even under seemingly homogeneous circumstances (Long 2001: 11 – 21 and Long 2002: 3). The constructivist approach, which considers that social reality is constructed and not given, is another cornerstone of an actor-oriented analysis (Long 1992: 25 and Long

2002: 3). Based on this fact Long (1992) developed the concept of 'social actor' which explains that people's lives are socially constructed (Long 1992: 25). Based on this perspective, 'constructivism' and 'heterogeneity' remain as a central concern in the analysis. The 'constructivism' approach touches consequently on the notion of agency and its theoretical importance. The analysis explains how 'heterogeneity' is generated and exposes its causes and effects on the groups of women under study.

The social position of these women as migrants necessitates analysis of how they cope in the new location in which they are experiencing a new working atmosphere. The study offers an empirical analysis of the ways women acquire information about and actually find work opportunities. It also lays emphasis on work negotiations and draws attention to work negotiations in the frame of gender relations. Another area of concern analysed by the study is that of the strategies and social practices applied by women via their social networks and, through which, struggles and problems in the work sphere are managed.

The analysis also underlines how these women, by means of their social networks, cope to solve the problems arising within their private sphere. Hence 'traditional social security' is considered as a key concept on which the analysis is based. The construction of 'traditional social security' represents a cornerstone in the cultural constitution of the women migrants. Furthermore, the analysis lays emphasis on the social isolation reported within the ethnic groups having a rich organizational life.

1.3 Layout and details of the chapters

This first chapter offers an introduction that shades light on the background of the study. It spells out the problem in context and rationale of the study. It highlights the general focus of the study and its achievements. It also presents the layout of the chapters, which encompasses delineation of each chapter. The second chapter presents to the reader an overview of the Gezira Scheme (GS), which covers different issues. In defining the Gezira Scheme, the chapter presents a historical perspective of the scheme and its human resources, essentially providing detailed information on the social and ethnic profile of the population. It gives a short overview of land ownership. Special emphasis is laid on the mobilisation of the agricultural labour force within the various labour regimes, highlighting the categories of labour force reported in the literature as well as the labour input. Social services are introduced, with special attention to those in the migrants' camps.

Since the focus of the study is on women and particularly women migrants, it is crucial to give the reader an idea of historical trends towards women's labour and migration, with emphasis on the causes of their migration. The current situation of women's labour is highlighted, with special emphasis on the forms of women's labour observed during the empirical research for this study. Looking into the pillars of the social structure of the migrant communities in the Gezira Scheme, it is clear that men are also involved in agricultural work. This necessitates a description of women migrants' work as parallel to that of men migrants, which indicates the significance of the gender division of labour. Finally, this chapter delineates the issue of women's land rights. These are the issues covered by chapter three.

The following chapter is mainly on the theoretical and methodological approaches. The fundamental aim of this chapter is to spell out the theoretical and methodological issues central to the collection and analysis of the empirical data. It defines the concept of social networks and outlines the approaches and the framework for analysing the empirical data. Hence, the intension of this chapter is to: 1/ highlight the perspective of social networks as well as the theoretical considerations and the type of social networks that are used by the study and; 2/ draw the theoretical notions and methodological issues found to be useful as an analytical dimension for the empirical data, instead of focusing on the prodigious literature on social networks theory and analysis and; 3/ discuss the research process which covers: the localities of the empirical research as well as the ethnic groups within each local, how the empirical research is done, my sojourn among the migrants in my home land plus my impressions and; 4/ outline the analytical framework, which entails the two realms of work and women's private spheres.

The next four chapters are exclusively analysis of the empirical data. Chapters five and six focus on the work sphere while chapter seven examines the women's private sphere. Chapter eight introduces two case studies. Chapter five attempts to discuss in detail the issue of the procurement of work opportunities. This entails examining social network processes that include information diffusion and work negotiations, aiming at studying how women find work opportunities. In particular, it explores the ways in which women get hold of information about work opportunities; either of sharecropping, land subleasing or wage labour. These means of information flow are traced in terms of how women acquire information about work opportunities in the Gezira area before migration from their place of origin and also how the process of information transfer operates after the women's migration.

In addition, the study identifies those who provide women with the information plus the circumstances under which they pass it on. The chapter lays special emphasis on the different ways of undertaking women's work negotiations through social networks. Furthermore, it draws attention to the nature of ties between women and the contact persons who undertake their work negotiations. The analysis also highlights the work negotiations in the frame of gender relations and the gender order. The importance of these areas of network research in this chapter is to explore the role that the social networks of women play in acquiring information and in the work negotiations. Furthermore, the analysis underlines the work relations with special emphasis on conditions under which the partnership (mainly sharecropping) continues or discontinues on the grounds of the respondents' perception.

Chapter six lays special emphasis on the analysis of women's strategies. It spells out the ways in which different groups of women as social actors manage, through social networks, to resolve problems in their work sphere. This necessitates analysing women's strategies in the work sphere, which are identified as diverse social practices and traditions carried out collectively by migrants, mainly women. This becomes more interesting when one looks at most of the women migrants ethnically, as non-original Sudanese within the Gezira Scheme social context.

Social practices of the migrants' communities are characterized by collectivities. Collective actions, togetherness and social solidarity are noticeable features among groups of migrants supporting each other in their work sphere. One should note that there is variety of social practices undertaken by each 'cohesive group'. Women are active participants and a compelling force in collective work in the field. These social practices and collectivity cover: 1/ *'Musaada'*, 2/ *'Nafeer'*, 3/ collective harvest and 4/ social interactions with the in-laws.

The same chapter also focuses on the analysis of the sources and effectiveness of women's collectivity and reciprocal social solidarity. I here argue that, despite the reality of existing cooperation and reciprocal social solidarity among women migrants, there are differences in the features of their social organizations and in the degree of their mutual help and reciprocal social solidarity. Based on this argument, the challenge that faces the analysis is to interpret the question of differential responses; why for instance some women who belong to a specific ethnic group practice more solidarity and close social interactions, enabling them to resolve their problems more than others. In other words, why are some women more differentiated and diversified than others? Such analysis explores the ethnic differences between the migrants groups under study. It is also crucial to examine the effectiveness of the existing forms of collectiveness and solidarity on the women migrants.

Chapter seven presents the analysis of all issues related to the women's private sphere. Women's private sphere signifies that women's building of social networks is constructed in a social world of their own. The analysis therefore examines how women belonging to each 'cohesive subgroup' of migrants attempt to create a private sphere in order to construct a social world that may run parallel to that of men. The structure of the analysis in this chapter necessitates consideration of 'social security' as a key concept. 'Social security' is examined in terms of women's informal associations as strategies for security and mutual social support in social occasions. The analysis also emphasizes women's 'social security' in the context of inter-household relations. The introduction of two case studies, essentially in chapter eight, covers the issue of social isolation within a single 'cohesive subgroup' of rich organizational life. The final chapter outlines the conclusion of the study. It reports outcomes of the study in terms of presentation of the main findings of the analysis of the empirical research on the issue under study. It presents additions to the previous theories and the new contributions proposed by the study.

2. The Gezira Scheme: an overview

2.1 The Gezira Scheme: a historical background

'The Gezira', is an Arabic name meaning 'the Island'. The Gezira Scheme (GS) is considered as the most important development project throughout the history of the Sudan and one of the largest irrigation schemes in the world. For over 80 years, the Gezira Scheme has been of central importance to the economy of the Sudan. It is located between the Blue Nile and the White Nile towards their confluence and to the south of Khartoum. (See: figure 1).

Figure 1: Sudan map and research area

First incepted as an experimental farm of 2000 feddans[1], it soon grew in size and was well established in 1925/26 when the Sinnar Dam across the Blue Nile was completed. The relatively flat land area, with inclinations from north to south and east to west, greatly facilitated the gravity irrigation system. Under the 1959 Nile Waters Agreement between Sudan and Egypt, which superseded an earlier 1929 agreement, one third of the total Nile waters was allocated to the Sudan. Of this amount about 85% is almost all used for irrigation purposes, much of it in the Gezira Scheme (Barnett & Abdelkarim 1991:1 and essaybank.co.uk: 1).

The Scheme was established by the British colonial rule in the Sudan (1898 - 1956) with the aim of producing cotton as a mono-crop for the British textile industry and also providing revenue for the administration of the quasi-colony. The National government, after independence (1956), designated social development as one of the main objectives of the scheme. In 1959-63 the original Gezira scheme was extended to include the Managil area. The combined Gezira Managil Scheme covers a command area of about 2.1 million feddan (about 882,000 hectares) under gravity irrigation. This area constitutes 12% of the total area cultivated in the Sudan and represents about 50% of all irrigated area drawing water from the Nile system. Originally, under British colonial rule, the area produced raw cotton for export to the textile factories in the United Kingdom. After independence, production was diversified. Out of the total land under irrigation, 1.5 million feddans per year are cultivated, on a crop rotation basis. Out of these, 350,000 feddans are for cotton, 400,000 for wheat, and the same for sorghum; 240,000 for ground nuts; 50,000 for vegetables; 10,000 for fodder, and the same for sunflowers; and 400,000 lie fallow (essybank.co.uk: 1).

The GS makes a major contribution to the national economy. It produces about 65% of the total country's production of cotton (for export), 70% of the country's production of wheat (for export and local consumption), 12% of sorghum and 15% of groundnuts for domestic consumption (Hagar 1996:14-15, Word Bank, 2000:1-2 and O'Brien, 1980:149). However, the World Bank report (October 27, 2000) reads; the Scheme has been plagued over many years by serious water management and distribution problems, as well as low yields, costly pest control for cotton, inadequate financing and marketing arrangements for most crops, inefficient agricultural processing, disillusioned farmers, and low cost recovery for irrigation water deliveries. As a result the GS regularly incurs an op-

[1] One feddan = 1.038 acres = 0.42 hectares.

erating loss and tenants often find it impossible to make ends meet from farm income alone despite the fact that the average farm size is 20 feddan. Since the Sudan's future agricultural trading opportunities would be linked to highly competitive global markets and if the GS is to play a major role in the Sudan economy, the search for strategies and policies to improve the efficiency of the Gezira has become more urgent (World Bank 2000:1-2).

2.2 Administration

The original design of the GS envisaged centralised management. The Scheme was established, according to official terminology, on a "partnership" basis, the three partners being the Government of the Sudan, which provided the land and irrigation (land was either confiscated, bought or leased from the original owners); the administration of the Scheme (the Sudan Plantation Syndicate, a private British company, replaced in 1950 by the Sudan Gezira Board (SGB), a parastatal corporation) and the tenants (O'Brien 1980: 207). In practice, this partnership was never arranged on an equal basis. Despite the fact that the Farmers' Union has been in existence since 1963/64 and some members of this union represent the tenants in the Gezira Board of Directors, this representation has had very little effect on the operation or planning of the Scheme. The tenants' representatives on the Board were only able to influence the relative shares of the partners within the Joint Account System[2] but, since the application of the Individual Account system[3] in 1981, even this degree of control has been removed from them (Barnett & Abdelkarim, 1991:21, and Barnett, 1977). This implies that decisions by the Gezira Board do not reflect strong leadership on fundamental issues. It is also worth mentioning that, although women tenants belong to the Gezira local community, they are never represented in the Farmers' Union. This can be attributed to the fact that norms and traditions bar the women from the luxury of such representation.

---

2 The Joint Account: A system of equal distribution of the cotton profit to the tenants, under a partnership basis (i.e. sharing arrangements of the production relation), among the three partners of the Scheme. The charges made to the Joint Account include the total charges of cotton for all the tenants.

3 The individual account: In this system each tenant is charged individually i.e. the profit of each tenant is calculated by deducting the cost of production of each tenant from his / her own product value under the partnership basis of the Scheme.

2.3 Human resources: social and ethnic profile of the population

The creation of the GS altered the composition and traditional social organisation of the area as the Scheme, since its inception, has attracted diversified ethnic groups from some other parts of the Sudan and non-Sudanese groups from West Africa.

The Central region where the GS is located has a high density of human habitation, particularly within the GS, where the total population is estimated to be about 2.7 million people, who depend on the scheme for their livelihoods. The majority of habitations are assigned to permanent residences while dwellings/camps associated with the migrant population are relatively rare. The permanents residents are tenants, traders, civil servants or work as agricultural family and hired labourers, while the migrants are principally agricultural wage labourers or share croppers. The core of the population is made up of about 114,000 tenants in the GS with an associated population of about 798,000, who by law must all be Sudanese. The average size of the household is estimated to be 7 persons. The migrant labourers live in about 1,000 camps with a population estimated to be about 600,000 (GRPMU & IDCA 1994: 1, and; WB, 2000: 38).

Ethnically the permanent residences are homogeneous as Sudanese ethnic groups belonging to the northern and central parts of the Sudan occupy them. The dwellings are heterogeneous, as they are occupied by migrants belonging to Sudanese and non-Sudanese ethnic groups. The Sudanese migrant labourers are originally from Darfur, with also a significant number from Kordofan.[4] In 1929, the majority of non-Sudanese migrant labourers in the Gezira were from West (namely Nigeria) and Central Africa. By 1954, it was estimated that that 16 percent of the Gezira population was made up of labour migrants from Nigeria and Chad, whereas some of the current inhabitants in the camp areas are originally from Darfur and Kordofan. This can be attributed to the dramatic influx from these areas to Gezira following the drought and desertification disaster in the 1970's and early 1980's, which was followed by the 1984-1985 famine (WB, 2000:38).

It is clear that the Scheme has drawn diversified groups of Sudanese and non-Sudanese people whose lives are intertwined with the Scheme land and therefore

[4] Darfur and Kordofan are regions located in the Western part of the Sudan. After the application of the federal system in the Sudan each of the two regions was divided into two states (north and south).

it has played a key role in transforming the socio-cultural, ethnic and economical texture of society in the whole Central Sudan.

2.4 Land ownership

Before the establishment of the GS, it was a common belief among the Sudanese that land is common for all, no private or public property. The people became aware of the term "Land Ownership" and the seriousness of the problem of land only after the Anglo-Egyptian rule in Sudan (Condominium Rule; 1898 - 1956). Land in the Gezira plain was used for rainfed crops and grazing under a land tenure pattern that included private ownership. During the period 1907 to 1910, the Government surveyed all the land in the irrigated area including Gezira and it was distributed to the tenants on rental basis. In 1921, the land ordinance was put into force. Under this ordinance, the Government either leased or bought land from its landowners. (Yousif 1997: 47 and; WB 2000: 40). This indicates that the privately owned land was compulsorily leased by the Government and put under the administration of the Sudan Plantation Syndicate (Hagar, 1992: 9). As a result, 60% of the land is today government land. The remaining 40% is still privately owned. Restrictions were placed on the sale and rent of freehold land to others (WB, 2000: 40).

2.5 Mobilisation of the agricultural labour force: a process of free labour formation

The method of labour mobilisation takes different forms according to different socio-economic and political conditions, as well as to variation in time. "The main characteristic features of labour regimes[5] in the process of mobilisation are first, separation of the producer from the means of production. In this case, different mechanisms are used either to force labourers and remove them from their activities involuntary or gradually through economic coercion. The second major characteristic is the degree of freedom of labourers to sell their labour. When Karl Marx analysed capitalism, he called wage labour 'free' because workers own no means of production and are 'free' to sell their labour force as a commodity in the market without any form of coercion beyond the economic necessity of earning a living"[6] (Bernstein et al, 1992:186). Before discussing Bernstein's system of agrarian structure and the labour regimes, it is important to note

---

[5] The term labour regime refers to different methods of mobilising labour and organising it in production (Bernstein et al, 1992:186).

[6] For details on Bernstein's classification of the labour regimes, see Bernstein et al, 1992: 186 - 194.

that under the British colonial rule the intentions, which were in Sudan similar to some other colonies, such as India, were to exploit the labour and the natural resources of the Sudan for the provision of raw material supply to the expanding cotton industries in the metropolitan country. That is to say, to expand the domestic market for the sale of industrial products and to use occupied territory as a regular source of income through investment activities, capital drain and profit repatriation. Moreover, the British colonials had to resort to forced labour in order to construct infrastructures such as railway lines. The achievement of these objectives necessitated the displacement of pre-capitalist social information of a new agrarian structure that meant new labour types of regimes.
According to Adam F., 1987, the transformation was made possible through a number of processes, the most important of which were:
a. The introduction of a money economy and **b.** the development of the "cotton crop export economy". The outcome of this process was new types of labour regimes, other than those which prevailed in the pre-colonial period (Adam 1978 in Shaaeldin 1987: 22 -23). To digress, it is important to explore the process of labour force formation in the Gezira Scheme.
As was laid down in the Tenancy Agreement, the provision of labour was considered to be the responsibility of the tenants. It was believed that the tenant's households would supply the bulk of the farm labour. It was also recognised that at certain peak times (e.g. weeding and cotton picking) the tenants might need extra family labour, and the Tenancy Agreement of 1927 allowed for loans to be extended to the tenants for the provision of wage labour.
Contrary to expectations, the tenants' household labour (THL) has proved not to be the main source of labour in the Scheme. The earliest available documentation of this statement appeared in Culwick's report (1955), where it was established that THL has always been second to wage labour with respect to the proportions of labour input.

From the beginning, the supply of wage labour in the Gezira Scheme was both seasonal and settled. These were mainly "Westerners" coming from West Africa and Western Sudan. The establishment of the Scheme, on the other hand, from the beginning started a process of 'free' labour formation in the region of Gezira itself. In the allocation of lands in the Scheme priority was given to the landowners and their nominees. Apparently many land users were not offered tenancies (or did not want to settle in the Scheme as permanent cultivators). These consisted of pastoralists and cultivator groups who had used mostly the central area of the Gezira away from rivers, which were not privately owned, for grazing as well as occasionally for cultivation. Not restricting themselves to the same pieces of land every time, those groups of pastoralists and cultivators could not claim the right to land as required by British colonial authorities, and therefore were not offered priority in the allocation of tenancies. However, many of them might have rejected the settled life anyway. What matters here is that these groups were forced to move away from the Scheme area to the east and the west towards the Blue and the White Nile areas (the latter includes the Managil region), probably to share lands with people already living there. However, it seems that moving away affected the natural growth of their herds, and this, probably among other reasons, made them look for additional sources of income. They were easy to recruit as seasonal wage labourers; they needed work, and the Gezira and its people were not alien to them. From the early days of the Scheme, Arabs of the Blue and White Nile areas (including Managil) have supplied Gezira with a major part of its seasonal labour (O'Brien, 1980:149, 207- 8).

In addition to those groups mentioned above two other groups of people were sources of wage labour in Gezira after the establishment of the Scheme. The first group were landless people under bond relationship or those who had worked as sharecroppers. The second were independent peasants who were not qualified for a tenancy distribution. Some members of these two groups may have moved outside the Scheme as independent cultivators. Some others, who had no such alternative or for other reasons preferred to stay, had to sell their labour power in the scheme to secure subsistence. Apparently this group was small compared to that of migrant labour. With the growth of the Gezira tenant population and with the Scheme either being unable to offer lands or becoming unattractive economically as an alternative for a growing number of Gezira local people, many started looking for alternatives in off-Scheme farming activities within the region or outside it. Naturally, for a large segment of the population this involved selling labour power.

It can be concluded that the Scheme began a process of 'free' labour formation in the region, though a large number of the people who were given access to land did not actually work as wage labourers in the Scheme itself. From another perspective, in some other areas where the process of free labour formation began, the Gezira, by providing wage labour opportunities, may have played an accelerator role in that process (ibid: 150-155).

2.6 Categories of the labour force

Based on the above review of the process of the GS labour formation and also according to the settlement of some groups of the seasonal agricultural workers, the agricultural labour force of the GS was classified in the literature in the following broad categories:

1. Tenants: These are the main employers of labour in the Gezira Scheme.
2. Settled migrants: These are predominantly non-Sudanese workers.

Many of the West African migrants came through Sudan as pilgrims. Their settlement in Sudan was encouraged by the British authorities between 1929 and 1932 when many tenants abandoned their plots in Gezira due to the effect of the global recession, combined with cotton blights, to produce crises in Gezira. Some of them settled permanently. Most prominent among them were a number of respected religious teachers and healers. In the 20th century Takari (African migrants) migration to Sudan grew greatly in volume and its nature altered, as the bulk of the immigrants came to be made up of poor Hausa peasants seeking to escape the oppression of the Fulani aristocracy in Nigeria. During the last 20 years a number of the seasonal labourers and also migrants from the neighbouring country Tchad have settled in the Scheme area.

3. Seasonal labourers: The Western Sudan seasonal labourers went to Gezira during their subsistence agriculture off-season, as well as during the period of environmental hazards (low rainfall and locusts) and when animal prices were low. So, they went to Gezira to supplement their income as wage labourers. Some of those seasonal labourers were resident labour of Gezira origin and a few groups of the White Nile and Blue Nile Arabs.
4. Family labour: These are the members of the tenants' families (Ibid; Barnett & Abdelkarim, 1991:21).

2.7 Labour Input

It is clear that there is an exclusive use of labour from outside the tenants' villages. Their labour input is mixed with that of the labour of the villages. Based on the above classification of the labour force and according to Barnett and Abdelkarim's (1991) explanation of the GS labour use, four input mixes were apparent:

1. Settled migrants undertaking cultivation and irrigation while seasonal labourers take care of the harvest.
2. A few full-time workers from the resident-village labourers supplement the seasonal labour for the harvest. It is likely that the two groups have had a long relationship with the tenants. In the case of the village labourers there may be a

kinship relationship, which sometimes has an impact on the precision of the contact form between the tenant and the worker; however, it is not significant in creating changes in the wage rate.

3. The household labour is used exclusively but, since it is not sufficient, especially during the harvest time, it is, hence, supplemented by other labourers.

4. Use of large groups of people from the village, mostly during the harvest time. They are assembled on an ad hoc basis depending on the financial ability of the tenants (ibid: 29).

One should note here that the forms of labour and the labour input that I recognized during the fieldwork of this study are different from those reported in the literature mentioned above. This change can be attributed to the settlement of some of the seasonal labourers who then become involved in other forms of labour, an increase in the influx of migrants (especially women from Tchad who settled in the Gezira area and engaged in the labour force of the Scheme) and a reduction in the need for labour from outside the scheme. These new forms of labour will be explained in the next chapter when discussing women's labour force.

2.8 Social services and the social change

The GS from its emergence in 1925 until nationalisation had greatly succeeded in utilising human and material resources but, at the same time, it had failed to transform the life of the local population into a more developed pattern to coincide with the vital role it was playing in improving the national economy. During the early period between 1925-1950, the scheme did not attempt to supply social services to the villages of the Scheme and certainly not to the labour camps (Yousif, 1997:131). In the period after 1950, however, under the Joint Account System, two percent of the proceeds from cotton were allocated to cater for social services in the Scheme area. Under this arrangement the SGB provided most of the tenants' villages with a multiplicity of social services namely in the fields of education, public health, and popular mobilisation. These services were provided by the Social Services Department of the Gezira Scheme and greatly valued by the tenants. With the change of production relations and the introduction of the Individual Account System in 1981, there was no fund allocated to the social services. The Social Services Department was dissolved in 1983. This created a vacuum in the Gezira rural areas, particularly in the fields of education and health. There was a clear decline in access to health services such as clinics, midwifery training, dispensaries, nutrition and hygiene awareness training. This has had particularly negative consequences for the women and children, who were major beneficiaries of these services. However, the two percent from the cotton return is still being collected by the Farmers Union, but little of it goes on catering for social services for the tenants. More effort was made by the Blue Nile Health Project[7] to support social services; however, these services came to an end when this project was over (WB, 2000:118 and 114). It is worth mentioning that the Gezira State[8] is considered to have some of the best social services in the country and it is second only to Khartoum State, and the GS has been the most important contributor to this high standard. However, the quality of these services is threatened by the poor performance of the Scheme. The population in the labour camps lacking such services within the camps are increasingly demanding the use of these services, and this has produced additional pressure on them (Yousif, 1997:131 and WB, 2000: 114). Differences in welfare between social groups (namely the tenants and the different categories of agricultural labourers) have been a feature of the GS since its inception. These groups are dependant on each other through labour and sharecropping contracts. Some analysts argue that the income-based differences in welfare between the groups are accentuated by having different access to public social services and this therefore creates tension between them, while some others claim that there is a little or no tension (WB, 2000:iii).

2.9 Social services in the migrant camps

The migrants' camps or labour camps, as one could call them, are settlements without any form of basic social services; even drinking water and health services. The migrants live in disadvantageous socio-economic conditions. They use the contaminated water of the nearby canals for their daily needs and women fetch water from the nearby villages of the local community for drinking and cooking. It is reported by the World Bank mission (2000) that while the Social Services Department was in existence, it did not maintain a presence in the camps. It did serve the tenant villages but the residents of the camps rarely benefited from the village services (ibid: 118). It was noticed during the preparatory phase of the empirical research of this study, particularly during the survey, conducted among several areas of the Scheme, that the migrants have no access to the health services in their residences. Access to health services in the villages of the local community is not easy. Lack of transport means they go for long distances to receive basic health services in the clinics and dispensaries in these vil-

7 The Blue Nile Health Project is part of the World Bank Rehabilitation Project.

8 The Gezira State is one of the 26 Federal States of the Sudan and it is where the Gezira Scheme located.

lages. *"This coupled with the high costs, means that the majority of the camp population uses traditional healing for ailments and diseases."* (ibid).

Transportation facilities are not available in the migrant camps. Donkeys and carts are the only facilities for some of the migrants, whilst most of them go on foot for long distances or take the public transport available in the villages of the local community. Regarding, for example, education, the great majority of the camps' population is illiterate. Khalwa education is widely spread in the camps. The number of children from the camps receiving education in the villages is very small (ibid.). Along the same lines, Isikdag (1991) reached a similar conclusion; that the sharecropper households do not offer the same provision for education to their offspring as the tenants' households (Isikdag, 1991:136). This can be attributed to the fact that the sharecroppers who are in most cases camp residents have no access to schools within the camps to which they can send their children. This social reality is a reason that discourages most of the migrants from sending their daughters to study outside their residences. It is only recently, at least in the localities of the fieldwork of this study, that the migrants have started to send some of their boys and only a few of their girls to schools in the nearby villages.

Other studies conducted by the Socio-economic Department of the SGB indicate that 74% of the camps' residents are illiterate, 26% attend *'Khalwa'* education, less than 2% of children are enrolled in primary school, less than 0.5% in senior schools, and less than 6% receive adult education. Moreover, there are high rates of dropouts, particularly among girls, who drop out of school at the ages of 13-14 (WB, 2000:118). During the empirical research of this study it was found that illiteracy is widely spread among women, and men only studied *'Khalwa'* education.

3. Women in the Gezira

3.1 Historical trend towards women's labour

Women in the Gezira Scheme have long been conditioned by the traditional and cultural discourses of their societies governing women's and men's spheres, in which women are not allowed to leave their homes to work in the agricultural fields. Likewise, Alarifi (1976) pointed out that, at the inception of the scheme the socio-cultural environment in the Gezira degraded women's work in agriculture (Alarifi 1976 in Hagar 1992: 17). Moreover, the work of women in agriculture was not needed, as there was plenty of cheap migrant labour. In addition to that, Hagar (1992) argued, even if the agricultural work of women was needed it was socially unacceptable for women to work in the field with the hired labourers, considered as strangers. (Hagar 1992: 14). So, women were totally excluded from the mainstream of agricultural development. As a result of this, women were economically and socially dependent on men. Culwick, a social researcher who studied the human factor in the Gezira Scheme (1951-56), perceived the role of men in perpetuating the concept of female unemployment and the commitment of women to unemployment: *"to admit to earning money seemed to involve loss of face in the implied need for money or rather in the implied failure to secure a prosperous husband."* (Culwick 1956: 17). This implies that community norms and traditions bar women from working in agriculture over a long period of time. Culwick went further, stating that, *"given the ingrained habits of mind and the social values of these women, given their genuine shrinking from exposure beyond the narrow limits of their own conventions it must be conceded that to work in the Scheme fields under present conditions would be an ordeal for most of them, and that those who have to do it really deserve sympathy"* (ibid: 17).

This attitude has changed over time and women's engagement and importance in the agricultural labour force has become a noticeable phenomenon. This is attributed to several economic and socio-cultural factors which encourage women to enter the Gezira Scheme labour market. These factors can be summarised as follows:

- Involvement of migrant women in agriculture for a long time has changed the misconceptions and beliefs favouring women of the local community.
- Awareness-raising coupled with the spread of education as a result of the establishment of the project and also exposure to external cultures through different media.
- Education resulted in a reluctance of the tenants' sons towards agricultural work, as they were attracted to white-collar jobs. This opened up opportunities for women tenants, labourers and sharecroppers.
- Migration of men outside the project area in search of other sources of income during seasons of low productivity and low prices, resulting in low economic return and high debt. Men either migrate to urban centres or to the Arab oil producing countries.
- Change of production relations from the Joint Account System (JAS)[9] to the Individual Account system (IAS)[10] encouraged participation of women as family labour.
- Poverty and dislocated economic conditions induces women to enter the labour market to contribute to the maintenance of their families (WB, 2000: 131; Hagar Hagar 1996: 43-44 and; Elkarib et.al: 1996: 5).

From what has been mentioned, the engagement of the women migrants in the agricultural work has played an important role in changing the local misconception and cultural beliefs toward women's work outside their home. This important social and cultural change created by women migrants in the Scheme area, in addition to the choice of the women migrants as an analytical group by this study, necessitates at this stage a closer look at women's migration before an investigation of the current situation of women's labour.

[9] The JAS is a way of equal sharing of cotton profit between the tenants under the sharing arrangements of production relation between the three partners of the Scheme (Adam, 1996:30). The charges made to the Joint Account include the total charges of cotton for all the tenants. This means that the profit is distributed to the tenants on an equal basis regardless of who produces what.

[10] The IAS is a way of charging tenants separately. This system is aimed at motivating the tenants to increase crop- production. The net profit would go to the tenant after deduction of all individual costs of production from his / her own product value. The costs of production beside others, e.g. fertilisers, include land and water charges which are considered as a source of finance to the administrative budgets of the SGB and the Ministry of Irrigation (Yousif, 1997: 225 and Adam, 1996: 30).

3.2 Women and migration

Migration has taken place in the Gezira area for more than seventy years. A delineation of different forms of migration in the history of Gezira affirms *"migration was not just reserved for men, as so much of the literature on migration has taken for granted"* (s Chant & Radcliffe 1992: 1-29 in Santen & Schaafsma 2000: 21). Women's migration to the Gezira' area is based on different reasons. Ecological, economic, social and political constraints are significant causes of women's migration. Women's migrant history reveals the strong link existing between life crises, kin ties and women's decision to move to places where support from family members or co-ethnics can be relied on (Knörr & Meier 2000: 15).

Migration to the Gezira is bound to historical, economic and ecological political events. Migrants (women and men) of diverse of ethnic groups, either originally Sudanese or non-Sudanese, settled in the Gezira Scheme area. Those originally non-Sudanese migrated from West Africa from Nigeria and Tchad. Fellata and Hausa are two ethnic groups of migrants who migrated from Nigeria and both are known among the Sudanese people as Fellata. Bargo, Tama and Beni Halba are ethnic groups that migrated from Tchad. The Sudanese ethnic groups migrated from the West of Sudan, either from Darfur or Kordofan regions. Fellata used to come through the Sudan on their way as pilgrims to *'Mecca'*. They migrated to the Gezira Scheme under the influence of the British colonial rule in Sudan (1898-1956). Hausa came to the Gezira escaping from the oppression of the Fulani aristocracy in Nigeria. Bargo, Tama and Beni Halba migrated to the Gezira because of the civil war in Tchad and the drought and desertification in the early 80's, in addition to social reasons. It is important to stress here that migration of women from Tchad, in addition to the first two causes mentioned, is a function of inter-relating; joining the husbands and relatives who preceded them to the Gezira. It is also attributable to the need for women's engagement in the Gezira Scheme labour force as a gender associated activity.

According to Radcliffe (1986) the African extended family structure is a primary influencing factor in the mobilization of family members in migration (Radcliffe 1986: 37). The settlement of different families belonging to one ethnic grouping in the same compounds in the Gezira Scheme is attributable to the strong contacts between the predecessors and those in the region of origin; a feeling of belonging; and a desire to be together.

Women migrants under study attributed the reasons for their migration to a variety of factors such as poverty, drought, civil war and a desire to join their relatives. Women migrants of Sudanese or non-Sudanese origin migrate with their families or relatives. At least one male guardian must accompany women on the route of migration women should be accompanied by at least one male guardian for social and cultural reasons. Women and men migrant respondents in the empirical research of this study explain that migration of women without male guardianship is not acceptable by their cultural discourse. This is conceived by the migrant communities as a taboo. They justify the company of men for support and protection as a mode of a gender order which the migrants conceive as a form of tradition.

3.3 Current situation of women's labour

Currently, women in the Gezira carry out diversified roles and portfolios. The participation of women as labourers has become very significant. According to what is reported in the literature, women's labour in the Gezira Scheme is split into the following groups:

1. **Women tenants:** These are women who own land. Women tenants are also divided into two subcategories. The first one includes women who work in their tenancies themselves. The other subcategory includes those who do not work on their land themselves either because they are from wealthy families, old or disabled. Mostly male relatives work the tenancies for them; sometimes they only supervise and manage work while relying on hired labour for the agricultural operations.
2. **Family labour:** This is unpaid labour in which women work on fathers', husbands', or brothers' land, considering it family ownership.
3. **Migrant wage labour:** This is wage labour that migrated from West Africa and settled in permanent camps in the project area. Women of this group spend half of the year participating in all agricultural operations as wage-workers. They also practice sharecropping with tenants on a large scale in groundnuts and vegetable production. 55% of those women also sub-lease portions of land from tenants. It is reported that the tenants trust them more than their male counterparts.
4. **Seasonal wage labour:** This category consists mostly of migrants from Western Sudan who seek off-season jobs for income supplement for their subsistence agriculture in their areas of origin. It is estimated that 80% of seasonal labourers are women. They are considered as the mainstay of cotton picking and ginning. They are also engaged in harvesting groundnuts and vegetables. (El-karib A. et.al. 1996:5-6 and Hagar 1992:17 and WB 2000: 131).

Current forms of women's labour:

The forms of women's labour that I recognized during the fieldwork of this study are different from those reported in the literature, e.g. by Hagar 1992 and 1994, Elkarib 1996 and the WB 2000. The following is my own classification:

1. Women tenants: Those are women who own the land in the tenancy-based system of the Gezira Scheme. They are women of the local community who are originally from Northern Sudanese ethnic groups.
2. Family labour: This is unpaid labour, most of whom are young women working on the tenancies of the men in the household.
3. Sharecroppers: Those are women who work as partners of the tenants in a sharecropping system. Sharecropping is a form of partnership-based system (of cropping) applied in the Gezira Scheme between the tenant and the partner who owns no means of production. It is applied in the cultivation of sorghum and groundnuts. The tenant provides the partner, who does all the hard work in the field, with the land and the initial ploughing of the land. The two of them share the sum of all other expenses, which are the costs of seeds and fertilizers, combine harvester rental, water taxes and *'Zakat'*. At harvest time and after the deduction of taxes, the net output of the product is divided equally between the tenant and the partner. The majority of the tenants' sharecroppers belong to: 1/ Bargo, Tama and Beni Halba ethnic groups originally from Tchad. 2/ Fellata and Hausa ethnic groups who migrated to Gezira area from Nigeria. 3/ A few ethnic groups from the Western part of the Sudan.
4. Land sub-leasers: They are from the same groups of people who do the sharecropping. (The local name of land subleasing is 'Dangada'). The tenant rents out part of the tenancy annually to the sub-leaser.
5. Wage labourers: These are cotton pickers and thinners who are mostly women from the migrant groups and few women from the poor families of the local community.

The women migrants constitute 90% of the last three categories, that is, sharecroppers, land subleasers and wage labourers.

3.4 Labour input: women's work versus men's work: a gender division of labour

For the purpose of understanding women's social networks, it is important to highlight at this stage women's work conditions before analysing other aspects related to their social networking, particularly in the work sphere.

Women's work condition is described here as the kind of work that different women's groups carry out in the field parallel to the work of male counterparts, which highlights the concept of gender division of labour. The framework for work in the field is set by the prevailing construction of gender in the social context of the Gezira Scheme. Most of the tenants are men whilst women are only 12% of the total number of the tenants (Hagar 1992:15). The, mostly old, women tenants rely on their male relatives to manage their tenancies. With the exception of a few female labourers and young women from the poor families who pick cotton as a source of income, the rest of the women of the local communities do not work in the agricultural fields.

Most of the agricultural work in the fields is certainly done by the migrants, the women migrants carrying out the bulk of this work. This is attributable to the fact that the life of women migrants is articulated by steady residence in the Gezira scheme whereas the male migrants are involved in either agricultural or non-agricultural activities. Those who are engaged in the latter activities work in the cities. Migrated men remain among their communities for relatively short periods during which their labour is required. The opening of the irrigating canals at the beginning of the agricultural season is a standard male activity. They also join women during the harvesting time for sorghum and groundnuts where the gender division of labour is maintained. Women migrant labour is the mainstay of wage labour in the cotton fields in which they carry out weeding, thinning and cotton picking. Since they also work as sharecroppers and land subleasers, they do all the agricultural operations pertaining to groundnuts and sorghum from sowing until the harvest. Vegetable production is also considered as men migrants' work, while the harvesting of vegetables is regarded as women's work. Regarding domestic work, women migrants shoulder all the responsibility, doing all the housework. Fetching of water for domestic uses from the canals as well as from the pipes in the villages of the local community is regarded as a standard women's responsibility. According to African culture, since this activity is classified as domestic work, it is *"perceived as an unalterable gendered division of labour"* (Padmanabhan 2002: 150).

3.5 Women's land rights

"It is evident that while the nature of the structural problems that limited or even blocked the effective implementation of agrarian reform varied in African countries one common constraint was a failure to include the issue of gender relations. In other words, all the reforms ignored inequalities embedded within the household and failed to recognise women as a significant element of the agricultural labour force." This was a concluding remark of the seminar on rural development in Africa in Algiers, 1982. According to Hagar (1992) despite the fact that the settlement of the Gezira Scheme was different from agrarian reforms in other African countries in that there was no feudalism or landlordism in the Gezira Scheme, they all met in marginalizing women and their roles. However the socio-economic condition in the Gezira area justified this attitude (Hagar 1992: 13).

Tenancy ownership, size and allocation:

Tenancy in the GS denotes ownership of a plot of cultivable land on lease from the Government according to the Gezira Land Ordinance of 1927[11] and as stated in the standard condition of tenancy 1936. Since the tenancy is by law a Government property it is not an ownership of land. The Gezira Land Ordinance of 1921 reads: "the tenant may not transfer, assign, sublet or part with the possession of the land comprised in the tenancy or any interest therein or in the crop grown thereon, except with the consent of the Government or such person or persons as the government may appoint as aforesaid". A farmer is also not allowed to own more than one tenancy. A tenancy can be inherited, but officially it can only be fragmented to half the size of a full tenancy. According to Hagar (1992) despite the fact that a tenancy can be inherited, inheritance of tenancies is not governed by the *'Sharia'* but by the Rules and Regulations of the Gezira Scheme (ibid: 9 and; WB 2000: 40).

In the case of women, there are a lot of restrictions concerning land ownership. This is represented in the rules of transference of the land of a deceased tenant. These rules do not safeguard the right of the widow to the tenancy of her husband. The block inspector, the block production council and the family of the deceased tenant are the ones who meet and reach consensus on to whom the land should be transferred. The brothers of the deceased tenant are, in most cases, unwilling to transfer the tenancy to the widow. The result is that there is only a small number of women able to acquire land through inheritance or purchase. They are only 13,000 female tenants in the Scheme, representing 12% of the total number of tenants (107000) (Hagar, 1992:15 and Hagar 1996: 41). Despite the fact that this ratio is much better than those of many of the Third World

---

11 The Gezira Land Ordinance of 1927 is an amendment of 1921 and 1923 ordinances.

countries, it does not address the significant participation of women in agricultural work, as paid or unpaid family labour or as wage labour, and which qualify them to own land. There is another limitation on the access of women to land ownership. The GS regulations and rules put them in a similar position to the under-aged. Hagar (1992) pointed out that women and the under-aged are given ownership rights only if male relatives are nominated as responsible tenants on behalf of women and if a male relative, in the case of the latter, is obliged to run the tenancy until they are old enough (Hagar 1992: 10). The case of the Gezira is not a unique one. It is more or less similar to the case of the gender inequality in the system of the land tenure of China where land, as pointed out by Zhu and Jiang (1993), is distributed to the farmers on the basis of village communities and according to the household size. Land tenure is controlled by contractual entitlements. Land contractors in village communities are households' heads, mostly men (Zhu and Jiang 2001: 204-205). This implies that women join the households of their husbands or other male relatives.

On the other hand, the social position of the women under study as migrants does not allow access to the tenancies because, according to the regulation of the land tenure in the Sudan, the tenancy should only be given to those of Sudanese nationality. While Hagar (1996) reported that women migrants lack any opportunity at all for acquiring land (Hagar 1996: 41) this study during the empirical research came across a few cases of women tenants from Fellata and Hausa. This is attributable to the fact that these two ethnic groups were the first ones to migrate and settle in the Gezira area, a few of them, mostly the third generation of these migrants, were afforded access to the tenancies either through inheritance or purchase.

4. Social networks: theoretical and methodological approaches

4.1 An introduction

The fundamental aim of this chapter is to spell out the theoretical and methodological issues central to the collection and analysis of the empirical data. It defines the concept of social networks and outlines the approaches and framework for analysing the empirical data. Hence, the intention of this chapter is: 1/ to concentrate on the perspective of social networks and the theoretical considerations highlighting the type of social networks used by the study and; 2/ to draw on the theoretical notions of social networks theory and applications useful for the analysis of the empirical data instead of relying on the plethora of literature on social networks theory and analysis and; 3/ to lay emphasis on an actor-oriented perspective, an important approach on which the analysis is based; 4/ to discuss the research process which covers: the localities of the empirical research plus the ethnic groups within each locality, how the empirical research is conducted, my being among the migrants in my own home country in addition to my impressions and; 5/ to outline the analytical framework which entails two realms i.e. work and private spheres.

Instead of simply using one approach, the analytical framework assimilates different approaches and methods of analysis; a method which broadens and strengthens the analysis. Different theoretical notions of social network analysis and applications that motivate a qualitative analysis and interpretation of the empirical data are used. The analysis is also based on an actor-oriented perspective developed by Norman Long (1992, 2001) (See figure 2).

Figure 2: Theoretical approach

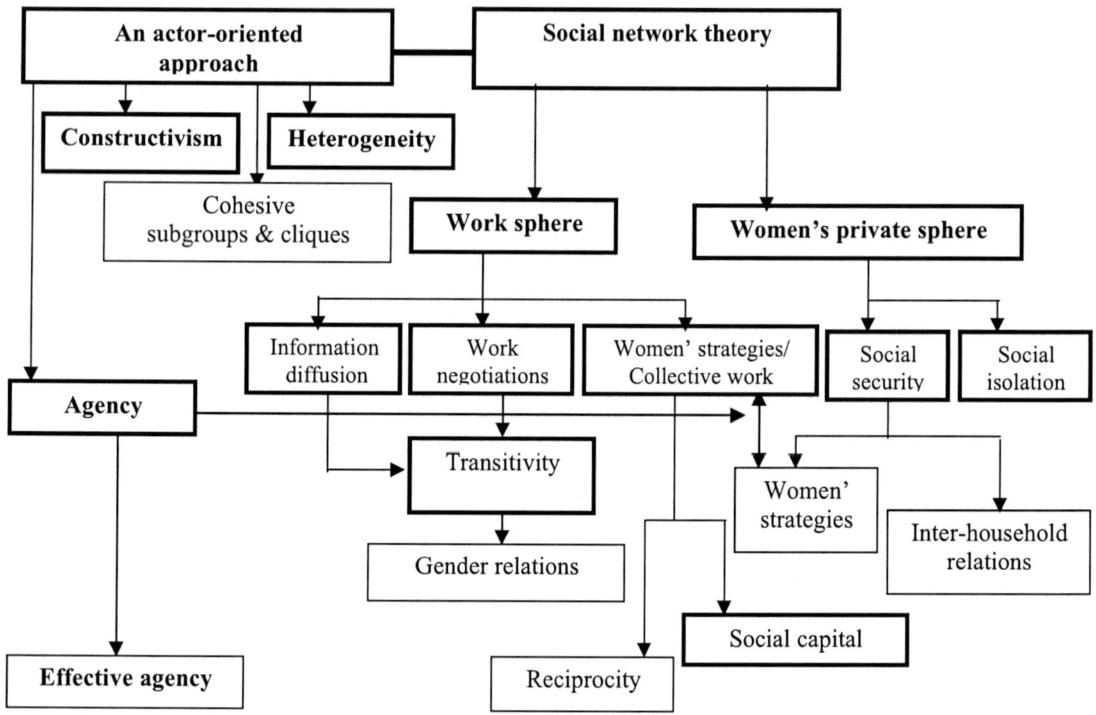

4.2 Social networks: perspective and theoretical considerations

The phrase "social network" refers to the set of actors and the ties among them. Ties can be any relationship existing between units: kinship, flow of resources or support, behavioural interaction or group co-membership. The relationship between a pair of units is a property of the pair and not inherently a characteristic of the individual unit. This signifies that the unit of analysis in network analysis is not the individual, but an entity consisting of a collection of individuals and the linkages among them. This demonstrates that social network analysis is a distinct research perspective within the social and behavioural sciences; distinct because social network analysis is based on an assumption of the importance of relationships between interacting units. These relations defined by linkages among units are a fundamental component of network theories (Wasserman & Faust 1994: 4 and 8 - 9).

Social networks researcher can only hope to learn about a fraction of a population, as shown by McCallister and Fischer (1983), since most people know hundreds of other people and have many different social networks from intimate kin to nodding acquaintances to vaguely familiar store clerks. One then ought to be explicit about the part of the network to be described and analysed (McCallister and Fischer 1983: 78). Based on the above perspective, this study seeks to depict social networks among the Sudan Gezira Scheme communities, taking women migrants as a central analytical group. It is the intention of the analysis to tap the respondents' (women's) networks that most influence their every day life. This is what McCallister and Fischer (1983) call "core" network and which they defined as the set of people who are most likely to be sources of a variety of rewarding interactions such as discussing work problem, personal problem, borrowing money or social recreation (ibid).

Given a collection of actors, the relational structure of a group or larger social system consists of the pattern of relationships among the collection of actors (Wasserman & Faust, 1994: 9). This gives the analysis, as Mark Granovetter (1973) calls, some "sense of community" which emphasizes that the unit of analysis is larger than a single individual (Granovetter, 1973: 1373) e.g. women groups, as in this study. Having Granovetter's "sense of community", one could then propose that the central debate of this study focuses on the ways of communal interaction, e.g. how women interact and how they cooperate and work individually or collectively to support one another.

Mitchell (1969) argues that it is a necessity to select particular aspects of the total network for attention. He conceptualizes these aspects as 'partial networks'. The partial networks studied by sociologists and social anthropologists are focused around particular types of social relationships. There are two bases on which such abstraction can proceed. First, there is the abstraction attached to particular individuals or groups of people so as to generate 'ego-centred' networks of social relations of all kinds. Second, there is the abstraction of the overall features of networks in relation to a particular aspect of social activity such as kinship obligations, or work relations (Mitchell 1969: 24 – 9 in Scott 1991: 31). Scott (1991) noted that Mitchell focuses on the second mode of abstraction as he recognizes the importance of its need to be anchored around particular individuals (or groups of people instead of individuals in this study) and also of its identification of partial networks by the 'content' or meaning of the relations involved (Scott 1991: 31). Based on this understanding, I found Mitchell's (1969) second base of 'partial networks' useful for women's social networks in the Gezira Scheme. This is because the focus of 'partial networks' around particular types of social relationships can be applied to the social networks of women migrants engaged in the agricultural labour force of the Gezira Scheme. In addition, the second abstraction of 'partial networks' necessitates a selection of specific aspects of social activity. These aspects are considered in this study as different kinds of social actions, social processes, social organisations and social obligations of these women migrants. In addition to that already borrowed from Mitchell's perspective, his distinction of structures of institutional relations, such as formal political and economic relations, from networks of interpersonal relations (ibid: 33) is also useful here since this study focuses on local social processes in terms of local actors' (women's) social networks.

4.3 Social network analysis: useful theoretical notions

The social network perspective encompasses theories and applications that are expressed in terms of relational concepts or processes. Therefore, the key feature of social networks theories is that they require concepts, definitions and processes in which social units or actors are linked to one another by various relations (Wasserman and Faust 1994: 4-5). Hence, it is worth taking some time at the outset to lay emphasis on the relevant theoretical notions and concepts of social network analysis and applications that can motivate the analysis and interpretation of the empirical data. These concepts are 'cohesive subgroup', formation of 'clique', 'transitivity', 'centrality', 'reciprocity', social capital, 'traditional social security' and 'social isolation'.

Wasserman and Faust (1994) define 'cohesive subgroups' as; subsets of actors among whom there are relatively strong, direct, intense, frequent, or positive ties (Wasserman and Faust, 1994: 249). This study makes use of the notion of cohesive subgroups of actors (women and men) in analysing women's social networks. This is not only because the concept of a 'cohesive subgroup' is one of the major concerns of social networks analysis, but also it is particularly necessary in the analysis of the migrants' communities in the Gezira Scheme. For the purpose of the analysis of women's social networks, a cohesive subgroup is defined as a subset of ethnocentric and/ co-ethnic group of migrants that lodge in one compound (a camp / periphery of a village). For more clarification, Seidman (1983a) writes, 'cohesive subgroups' "...in social networks have usually been seen informally as sets of individuals more closely tied to each other than to outsiders" (Seidman, 1983a: 97 in: Wasserman and Faust 1994: 267). Hence, the members of a 'cohesive subgroup' should be relatively more bound to one another when compared to outside ties. Thus, instead of concentrating simply on the properties of the ties among members within the subgroup, it is necessary also to compare these to properties of ties of actors outside the subgroup (Wasserman and Faust 1994: 267). Another concept associated with the notion of cohesive subgroups is a 'clique'. A 'clique' is a collection of actors all of whom "choose" each other, with no other actor in the group chosen by all members of the clique. The clique definition is a useful starting point for specifying the formal properties that cohesive subgroup should have (ibid. 254). This means that a 'clique' is a restricted definition of the 'cohesive subgroup'.

'Transitivity' as one of the notions of social networks analysis is found to be very useful here. 'Transitivity' is a property that considers patterns of trios of actors in a network (ibid. 165). Hence, transitivity is considered by this study as a form of indirect relations that operate through intermediaries. The statement by Wasserman and Faust (1994) that: *"...clusterability leads naturally to a consideration of transitivity"* (ibid. 243) drew my attention to the importance and usefulness of the 'transitivity logic' in the formalisation of women's social networks. This is because; settlements of the migrants and people of the local community in the Gezira Scheme are characterized by ethnocentrism, which means that those groups are distinctive as clusters. Hence, studying social network processes like information diffusion and work negotiations that operate through intermediation process provides an appropriate approach for discussing these processes through the application of the 'transitivity logic'. Furthermore, since these processes of information flow and work negotiations are mostly undertaken by means of 'transitivity', the significance of the 'weak ties' and their maintenance (ref. to Granovetter 1973) are useful in such analysis.

Granovetter applied the weak ties in the context the USA cities. These weak ties are between individuals who have no social contacts between each other because they do not know each other i.e. outside the social circles of each other. Empirical evidence by Granovetter shows that if there is no relationship between some individuals, their common strong (independent) ties to another person will bring them into interaction to generate a new relationship. The individuals who look for jobs use their common strong (independent) ties to another person, who might be a friend, who will bring them into interaction to generate a new relationship. Granovetter used the similarity as a detective factor to indicate whether the ties between selected individuals are strong or week (Ibid).

'Centrality' implies that the most important or prominent actors are usually located strategically within the network. It is important to describe the properties of 'actor location' in a social network (For more details see Wasserman and Faust 1994: 169). A curious irony of network research is that, despite its focus on the causal importance of structures of relations among actors rather than their properties, the research treats network positions as properties themselves. Thus, studies often regard network centrality as an essential feature of the social network. Centrality, however, has significance only in specific network contexts. The remedy for this matter proposed by Powel and Smith-Doerr (1994) is found useful here. It is to highlight the content of ties, rather than merely the structure formed by these ties (Powel and Smith-Doerr 1994: 371). Prominent actors are those who are extensively involved in relationships with other actors. This involvement makes their ties more visible to the other actors in the network (Wasserman and Faust 1994: 172 - 173). 'Centrality' is found to be useful in analysing the position of male migrants and tenants as different kinds of actor in work negotiations. Consequently, the usefulness of centrality in such analysis necessitates examining the way women migrants assign their male counterparts to undertake work negotiations.

'Reciprocity' as an important concept in social networks theory is found to be useful in the analysis of the women migrants' collective actions, social practices and social support. Scott (1991) pointed out that reciprocity is an important concept through which interpersonal networks can be analysed. 'Reciprocity' describes the quality of relations involved. Reciprocated relations involve ex-

changes, and so can be considered as 'directed' from one person to another (Scott 1991: 31 - 32). This also touches crucially upon the issue of reciprocal solidarity, found to be useful in the analysis of social actions and provision of labour resource and social practices.
Going further in seeking other useful analytical tools and notions that can be utilized in analysing the women's social networks, 'traditional social security' is found to be a fundamental analytical dimension. 'Traditional social security' can be defined as a women's "coping capacity" or "solidarity capacity", as Lachenmann (1998) calls it, in terms of their ability to cope with insecure living conditions (Lachenmann 1998: 7) is an important component of the analysis. Scott (1988) argues that the traditional 'social organization of safety' in African societies is characterized by generalized reciprocity and solidarity (Schott 1988). Construction of 'traditional social security' by the women migrants is examined in terms of women's mutual social support and the social obligations of sharing that women offer each other, as well as the strategies they apply to cope with their insecure economic and social conditions. Furthermore, the analysis highlights the 'traditional social security' which women construct in the context of household relations.

Examining social networks, social security draws attention to the examination of the converse 'social isolation'. The definition of 'social isolation' is founded on the causes that lead to its prevalence. The definition of social isolation, which fits this study, is derived from the definition in the Web (1). Social isolation is a *"feeling of aloneness experienced by the individual as a threatening state imposed by others; a sense of aloneness caused by the absence of family and friends"* (Definition in Web: www.birf.info/home/bi-tools/qlinks_s.html) in addition to a feeling of social distance and physical and mental displacement. Physical displacement is defined as being reallocated to a new place. Mental displacement is identified in terms of the feeling of being out of place in which the individual identity is challenged. Thus, social isolation is *"a lack of interaction or contact with individuals within one's social networks"* (La Veist et. al 1997: 723).

The concept of livelihoods as relating to the living conditions of the poor is found to be useful in the analysis of socially isolated cases among women migrants belonging to the same ethnic group. A livelihood in its simplest sense is a means of gaining a living. Capability means enabling the livelihood to be gained (Chambers and Conway 1992: 6). A livelihood comprises the capabilities, assets and activities required for a means of living. A sustainable livelyhood is one which can cope with and recover from stress and shock, maintain or enhance its capabilities and assets and provide sustainable livelihood opportunities for the next generation (ibid: 7-8). The concept of sustainable livelihoods relates to the living conditions of poor people, their opportunities and capabilities for well-being, their resilience, their activities required for a means of living, their resource bases (comprised of various assets) and their ability to cope with and recover from stress and shock (de Haan and Zoomers 2005 and ibid: 1992: 7).

4.4 Network membership

In social network research, individuals are identified and their direct and indirect link to others are traced (Scott 1991: 31). Borrowing Scott statement by this study, women groups instead of individuals are identified. As the findings of network research can be strongly influenced by what kind of "relation" is used to define the network as an important conceptual issue, attention should also be paid to the methods that are used to identify network memberships (McCallister & Fischer 1983: 87). Hence, the actors who are targeted by this study are the women migrants engaged in the agricultural labour force of the Gezira Scheme. They are women either of non-Sudanese origin who migrated to the Gezira area from West Africa (Tchad and Nigeria) or originally Sudanese who migrated from Western Sudan. The structure of the analysis of the empirical data is undertaken at the camp (i.e. settlement of the migrants) levels with their distinguishing ethnic groups, social status and categories of women's labour. It is noteworthy that the forms of women's labour that I recognized during the fieldwork of this study are different from those reported in the literature, as explained in chapter three of this study.

4.5 An actor-oriented perspective: an analytical dimension

The constructivist approach considers that social reality is constructed and not given. Based on this fact Long (1992) developed the concept of 'social actor' which explains that people's lives are socially constructed. The individual is transformed into a social actor, signifying that a social actor is a social construction rather than simply a synonym for the individual (Long 1992: 25). This study seeks to understand the construction of social networks of women migrants engaged in the agricultural labour force of the Gezira Scheme through which social forms and arrangements emerge, consolidated or reworked in the everyday lives (Long 2001: 49) of these women. This implies that the study analyses the social networks of women migrants in terms of heterogeneous social processes, social interactions and practices of different categories/groups of women migrants, and through which women construct their lives. Hence, 'constructivism' and 'heterogeneity' are important theoretical approaches to this study.

As to 'heterogeneity', which is linked to the alternative discourses that are available in people's social life, there is no better description than Long's (2001); social life is never so unitary as to be built upon one single type of discourse. However it restricts their choices, actors always face some alternative ways of formulating their objectives; organizing specific modes of action and giving reasons for their behaviour. This is manifested by the fact that all societies contain within them a range of different life styles, cultural forms and rationalities, which members utilize in their search for order and meaning and which they themselves play a part in affirming or restructuring. Hence, the strategies and cultural constructions employed by individuals are drawn from a stock of available discourses that are to some degree shared with other individuals, contemporaries and perhaps predecessors (ibid: 18).

The theoretical and methodological perspectives of an actor-oriented approach, developed by Long (1992 and 2001), offers valuable insights into those processes of social construction, as well as the heterogeneity. The actor approach enables explanation of different responses in similar structural circumstances, even if the conditions appear relatively homogeneous, a feature that reflects the meaning of 'social heterogeneity' (ibid: 11 and 21). Hence, this advantage of the actor-oriented approach specially suits the analysis of social interactions and different responses of women migrants in the Gezira Scheme whose social and economic conditions are more or less similar. Moreover, the analysis also deals with the question of differential responses; why for instance some ethnic groups practice more solidarity and close social interactions than others or, in other words, why some are more differentiated and diversified than others.

The main theoretical challenge facing this analysis is, therefore, to explain how 'heterogeneity' is generated and contained between different groups and within one group living in structurally similar circumstances (ibid: 21 - 22). An approach that then emphasizes the importance of analysing the different social interactions and social practices of women migrants belonging to each 'cohesive subgroup' and the differences and similarities between the social practices of the existing groups. Hence, differences in the forms of women's social organizations and in the degree of their (namely, the ethnic groups') social solidarity and mutual help are important issues to be taken into account. Furthermore, I argue that it is unsatisfactory to examine only the differences between the existing groups in the degree of their social solidarity. It is also significant to try to find out the causes of these differences between the comparable groups and their effects on each group as well. Thus, the question of heterogeneity will remain one of the central concerns in the analysis of the empirical data.

The actor-oriented approach also enables the conceptualisation of how local interactional settings interlock with wider networks of relations, thus facilitating a re-thinking of key concepts (ibid: 49) such as specific social practices. Using this approach gives significant attention to the multiplicity of all social actors involved in restructuring (ibid: 12) women's social networks. This perspective implies a concern for how various actors (women) organize themselves around the problems they face (Long 1992: 36). This goes beyond the analysis of economic and political aspects to analyse local social processes. These social organizations, therefore, emerge, as Long (1992) argues, as a set of social arrangements worked out between the parties concerned (i.e. women groups) (ibid). Such an approach is found to be useful in examining the women's everyday life experiences to understand their social networking, which is made up of a complex of actions and social interactions. These social interactions are the ones that are reproduced within and between the particular social groups of women targeted by the study and also between these women and men.

An actor-oriented perspective, as Long (1992) argues, entails recognizing the multiple realities and diverse social practices of various actors (ibid: 5). He carries the discussion further by asserting that no sociological study could be complete without a concern for the ways in which different social actors manage and interpret new elements in their lifeworlds, an understanding of organizing, strategic and interpretive elements involved and a deconstruction of conventional notions of planned intervention (ibid: 9 and 33 - 34). Borrowing Long's (1992) argument, an actor-oriented perspective necessitates a full analysis of the ways in which different social groups of women migrants manage and interpret new elements in their lifeworlds within the receiving context of the Gezira Scheme. Hence, using this perspective in analysing women's social networks necessitates placing each women's group at centre stage to analyse the social networks among each group and also among other women's groups.

The question of women's strategies is another important analytical dimension. Women's strategies are central to this analysis because it aims to interpret how women actively construct their social realities and everyday life to resolve their livelihood, and the work problems through their social networks within the limits of scarcity of resources and within the cultural discourse in which they operate their labour. Long suggested that an actor-oriented approach begins with the simple idea that different social forms develop in the same or similar structural circumstances. Such differences reflect variations in the ways in which actors attempt to come to grips, cognitively, emotionally and organizationally, with the situations they face and are not viewed as due to the impact of broad social forces e.g. ecological forces. (Long 2001: 20). One of the main tasks for analysis, then, is to identify how women by means of their social networks apply strategies through which struggles and problems at work and in their private sphere are managed. It is also a concern of the analysis besides the identification of women's strategies and rationales to consider, as noted by Long (1992), the conditions under which they arise, their viability or effectiveness for solving specific problems, and their structural outcomes (Long 1992: 27).

Furthermore, in examining women's strategies, their social practices and informal groups, the analysis will borrow the paradigm model of the axial coding of grounded theory. This is because this model includes causal conditions, social practices (instead of phenomenon), context, action and interactional strategies and consequences. These concepts are useful for the analysis of social networks since this model deals with actions and interactions. However, the analysis will use the concept of social practices instead of phenomenon (ref. to Straus & Corbin 1990: Chapter 7). In examining the causal conditions of a specific social practice it is important to be aware of two facts: a causal condition depends upon the situation and; in reality, a single causal condition rarely produces (ibid: 100) a social practice. Context is defined by the founders of the grounded theory (Straus and Corbin) as specific properties that pertain to a social practice, like the place of the event or incidence that related to (ibid: 101) a social practice; for example, where a specific social practice takes place (i.e. which community, how, who takes the decision for someone to participate and why, ...etc.). Context also represents a particular set of conditions within which the action / interaction strategies are taken to manage a specific problem. Those strategies are action oriented. They imply that groups or collectives take action / interaction- directed at managing and responding to a specific problem as it exists in specific context under specific set of perceived conditions (ibid: 101 and 105).

Resistance is an important concept related to the women's strategies. Dannecker, a German social anthropologist, studied the modes of resistance and networking as strategies of the women workers in the garment factories in Bangladesh. She analysed the tactics of resistance that exist beyond the household level. These exist inside the factories together with the attempts of collective actions (Dannecker 1999:1-2). The connection of resistance with networking fits in analysing the strategies of women migrants in the work sphere.

Since women's strategies are mostly considered as collective actions and productive activities within the social structure of the migrant communities, the notion of 'social capital' is found to be useful when analysing such strategies. During recent years, the concept of 'social capital' has become one of the most popular exports from sociological theory into everyday language. It has been applied to so many events and in so many different contexts (Portes 1998 and Thieme 2006: 49). Nevertheless, according to different scholars (e.g. Coleman 1988, Portes 1998, Pieterse 2000, Woolcock 2001 and 2003) who wrote on 'social capital', there is still no uniform conception of what is meant by 'social capital'. Despite these differences there is an emerging consensus in the literature concerning the definition of the concept, which can be summarised in the following definition: *"Social capital refers to the norms and networks that facilitate collective action and to its resources."* (Buchenrieder 2006: 6). It is important to note here that 'social capital' is defined by its function. It is not a single entity but a variety of different entities with two elements in common: they all consist of some aspects of social structures and they facilitate certain actions of actors whether persons or cooperate actors within the structure. Like other forms of capital, 'social capital' is productive, making possible the achievement of certain ends that in its absence would not be possible. Unlike other forms of capital, 'social capital' is inherent in the structure of relations between actors and among actors as a resource for them (Coleman 1988: S98). 'Social capital' facilitates productive activity. For example, a group within which there is extensive trustworthiness and trust is able to accomplish much more than a comparable group without that trustworthiness and trust (Ibid). According to Woolcock (2001) and Buchenrieder (2002 and 2006) Trust should be more accurately understood as an outcome of 'social capital' not a source. (Woolcock 2001 and Buchenrieder 2002 and 2006: 6).

The important forms of 'social capital' found to be useful in the analysis of this study in addition to using the general notion of 'social capital', are 'bonding social capital', 'Structural social capital' and, 'cognitive social capital'. 'Bonding social capital' refers to strong ties among people of close relations and who are similar in terms of their demographic characteristics, such as neighbours, friends and work colleagues. 'Bonding social capital' provides social support such as emotional or physical help in a crisis (Woolcock 2003). 'Structural social capital' refers to established formal and informal social networks that serve as platform for collective actions and decision-making (Buchenrieder 2006: 9). However, according to the function of the women migrants' 'social capital', formal social networks do not exist. This means that only informal social networks are considered. Several scholars claim that 'cognitive social capital' consists of shared norms, values, attitudes, perceptions of trustworthiness of other people, solidarity and beliefs. These factors predispose people toward mutually beneficial collective action. Compared to 'structural social capital', 'cognitive social capital' is difficult to observe.

'Bonding social capital' in the case of women migrants in the Gezira Scheme fits into the women belonging to their 'clique' or a single 'cohesive subgroup'. 'Structural social capital' in terms of informal social networks is useful in analysing the informal arrangements between women migrants belonging to different ethnic groups. 'Cognitive social capital' is used in analysing the characteristics that women belonging to different ethnic groups share e.g. shared values that foster these women, for example, to construct beneficial collective actions.

The social construction of women's life and strategies touches crucially upon the issue of agency. Consequently, the identification of 'agency' is a necessity as a notion of theoretical importance as well as taking into account the issues associated with agency. Giddens (1984) postulates that the concept of agency attributes to the actors the capacity to process social experience and to devise ways of coping with life, even under the most extreme forms of coercion. (Giddens 1984: 1 – 16; in Long 2001: 16). It is also useful here to consider the two principal elements of agency identified by Giddens (1986), 'knowledgeability' and 'capability' of social actors to monitor their own actions, to solve their problems and to intervene in the flow of social events around them (ibid). In addition to that, Turner's (1992) theoretical interpretation of social action that goes beyond Giddens' elements to embrace 'feelings, emotions, perceptions and identities' (Turner 1992: 91 in Long 2001: 18) is taken into account. Along the same lines as Giddens, Long pointed out that the social actors should be able to process the social world around them and upon which action takes place, a way which avoid the types of analysis that reduce questions of social actions to the performance of pre-dominated social roles or to the symbolic normative orders or social hierarchies (Long 2001: 16). This perspective suits: a/ one of the methodological instruments; that is, women's private sphere in which women construct their own social worlds (ref. to Long 1992: 24), explained later in this chapter; b/ the analysis of women as a gendered social group without restricting their social actions to, for example, women's triple roles. Furthermore, the concept of actor should not include collectivities or social categories that have no visible way of formulating or carrying out decisions (Hindess 1886 in Long 1992: 23). It is also decisive to emphasize here that 'agency' must not only be associated with the decision making ability but it is identified when particular actions make a difference to pre-existing situations, what is often referred to as 'effective agency'. Effective agency depends crucially upon the emergence of network of actors and requires strategic generation of a network of social relations and can only be effective through them (Latour 1986: 264 in Long 2001: 17 and Long, 2001: 17). It is therefore crucial to examine how women migrants as social actors by means of generation and manipulation of their social networks and by their decision-making processes and in constructing their lifeworlds develop and acquire some forms agency and/or 'effective agency'.

4.6 The research process and methodology

4.6.1 Approaching the Gezira as a researcher

Choosing the Gezira as my research location was different for me than approaching any other research site where I had previously worked. This is because the Gezira has lingered in my mind since my childhood when I used to spend my school vacations there. It was my parents' home. This social reality creates a special link between me and the Gezira area and its people. This link is associated with specific construction of kin relations, cultural background and memories. My choice to work among women emanates from my own concern about rural women, also associated with my academic background. My first university degree was a B.Sc. in Agricultural sciences in the Faculty of Agriculture, University of Khartoum (U of K), the second a post-graduate diploma in development studies in the Development Studies and Research Centre (DSRC), U of K and the third an M.Sc. in social sciences in which my option was Agricultural and Rural Development, in the Institute of Social Studies (ISS) of The Hague in the Netherlands. Added to that is my work experience in the Institute of Women, Gender and Development Studies of Ahfad University for Women (AUW) in Omdurman, Sudan. My fellowship with AUW as an institution, a pioneer in women's education and a university maintained exclusively for women, has strengthened my concern with women. The strategy of AUW is to provide women with skills and knowledge to become agents of change to assume leadership positions in society and to enhance women's status towards empowerment, development and full realization of their human capacities. Furthermore, my option to examine women's social networks on the ground of sociology originates, on the one hand, from my academic background in social sciences and, on the other hand, from my interest and objective to bridge the gap in social networks not featured in the discussion and analysis of rural Sudan.

During the fieldwork I visited the migrants camps in the Gezira Scheme on a daily basis. I lived in the women migrants' world, which was the central focus of my study. My gender made it easier for me to obtain insights into how women migrants experience their everyday life in the work sphere as well as in their private sphere. Despite the fact that this empirical research was not my first in the Gezira area, I could figure out the specificity and distinctiveness of this experience from the outset of the fieldwork. Conducting the empirical research among the migrants in the Gezira Scheme was a unique experience for me as a researcher inside my own homeland. Working among the migrants in the Gezira area is like working in *"a small Africa",* as Dr. Martina Padmanabhan[12] of Humboldt University of Berlin described the Gezira Scheme in one of our informal discussions. I was struck by diversity of ethnic groups from other parts of Sudan and from other African countries. In spite of my familiarity with the area, the social structure and the cultures, I discovered that I was exposed to a new and different experience when working in this *"small Africa"*. This work offered me a new and enormous experience in learning about a social world with its specific social structures, social and cultural discourses moulding the outlook of the people, and the forms and linkages of social networking. It was an opportunity to study women migrants' everyday life experiences different from the ones that I became familiar with in my earlier research. On these grounds, this fieldwork in the Gezira gave me an excellent opportunity to understand the functioning of women migrants' social networks and, at the same time, allowed me to learn about the meaning and roles, which these social networks have for the women migrants.

[12] Dr. Martina Aruna Padmanabhan graduated in Rural Sociology with a pronounced interest in gender studies, sociology of knowledge and participatory methodology. She gained vast empirical experience in Africa, as she did her Ph.D. in: Gender Relations and Agricultural Innovations in Northern Ghana (ref. to Padmanabhan 2002).

4.6.2 Choice of the fieldwork site

This examination of women's everyday life to understand their social networks is based primarily on qualitative research I conducted in two localities in the Gezira Scheme. Locality means a village of the local community and the surrounding migrant camps. Baika, the first village, was selected due to 1/ its importance in the Gezira Scheme as the main water canal, which comes from the Sinnar Dam, passes through Baika and splits into different canals to constitute the surface irrigation system of the whole Scheme and; 2/ Availability of the migrant camps around the village. The empirical research in this village is concentrated in two settlements of the migrants, occupied by two ethnic groups from Chad, called *'Bargo'* and *'Tama'*. The Bargo ethnic group occupies Dar Elsalam camp whereas the Tama occupy camp Number 7. (See appendix 3)

Elsoreeba, the second village, was selected due to: 1/ the collection and settlements of the migrants, different from those which surround the first village. This is attributable to the availability of migrants of diversified ethnic backgrounds; Sudanese that migrated from western Sudan and non-Sudanese, namely Bargo and Tama, originally from Tchad. They all stay at the periphery of the village. Another reason for choosing this village is the availability of a quite large settlement of migrants called Daim[13] Wad Ellaithie that lies nearby the village. It includes diversified ethnic groups who are originally Sudanese and non-Sudanese. The former group is called the Misairia who migrated from western part of the country and the latter includes the Fellata and Hausa ethnic groups, originally from Nigeria, and the Bargo, Tama and Beni Halba ethnic groups, who migrated from Tchad. (See appendix 4)

In light of the above, the selection of the villages is based on accessibility. Regarding the differences in the ethnic background of the women migrants, six ethnic groups of women respondents can be differentiated; Bargo, Tama, Beni Halba, Fellata, Hausa and Misairia. Hence, the analysis is mainly based on these six ethnic groups targeted by the research. Further, the analysis considers the difference between the compounds occupied by co-ethnic (i.e. same / one) group and the one- occupied by various ethnic groups.

Women's forms of labour are another grouping of the women migrants beside the ethnic background. Women migrants' labour encompasses various forms of

[13] Daim is a relatively old and large camp.

labour in the Gezira Scheme; sharecropping, land sub-leasing and wage labour. This does not mean that all women migrants operate all these three forms of labour at once (i.e. in one season), although some of them do. Some women work only as sharecroppers and/or land subleasers, a few of them work only as wage labourers (e.g. cotton pickers), while others perform the three forms of labour. Hence, the forms of women's labour appear in the analysis as a significant feature of distinction. From what has been explained, representation of women in the analysis is by contextualizes social strata. Representation depends on the contextualization in relation to ethnic group, age, age group, social status and forms of labour.

4.6.3 Eligibility criteria for selection of women respondents

The selection of the interviewees from the target groups of the women migrants is mainly based on the following three criteria:

1/ Enrolment of women respondents in one, two or all of the three categories of women migrants' labour in the Gezira Scheme: Sharecroppers, land subleasers and wage labourers.

2/ Belonging of the women respondents to the different ethnic groups of the migrant communities existing in the Gezira Scheme in order to give the research a multi-ethnic dimension. This is mainly to enable examining the social networks of women within each ethnic group and between different ethnic groups and to be able make a comparison between the different ethnic groups.

3/ Residence in the catchment villages of the local community or the migrant camps, a condition that guarantees the engagement of the respondents in the existing social networks.

4.6.4 Approaching the migrant communities

It was contrary to what I thought, and not easy- to approach the women migrants without full consideration of the 'African' patriarchal cultures. In my first visit to Dar Elsalam, occupied by the Bargo ethnic group, two women from Baika (the nearby village of the local community) accompanied me to that camp. One of those ladies works in the health centre as a nurse, and specialised in the vaccination of the children. Her choice as a counterpart was linked to her familiarity with almost all the women migrants in the surrounding camps who come to the health centre. Huda is the first woman migrant to whom I was introduced to in the camp. She used to be a sharecropper of the nurse' mother (i.e. a woman tenant). When I introduced the research and myself to Huda, we (my two companions and myself) realized that there were other steps we should take before I could commence my empirical research. Huda, who turned out to be my counterpart, said to me: *"We women could never work with you without permission from the Sheikh*[14]*"*. Accordingly, she accompanied us to the Sheikh's place. I explained to him the reason for my being in the camp. He agreed that I could start my work after he first announced to the men in the mosque; they, in turn, would relate the information to the women in the camp. Thus, from my first day in that camp I became aware of the availability of a different cultural discourse from that which I am familiar with in the Gezira area and of the centrality of the Sheikh. To me, this was a new experience which shows on the one hand how women and men migrants' social world relate to gender divisions. On the other hand it means a dichotomization between the academic discussion and social reality.

A more or less similar process was also applied to the other camps occupied by migrants from Tchad (Bargo, Tama and Beni Halba ethnic groups). Regarding migrants from Nigeria and from western Sudan, the case was different as there was no need to get permission from the Sheikh. My counterparts introduced me to them and then I commenced the empirical research.

Approaching the young women migrants as respondents was easier than approaching the old women. This is attributable to the ease of communication between the young women and me, as most of the elder women do not speak Arabic. The young women were a great help to me as they did simultaneous translation during the interviews of the elder women.

I was really struck by the high geographical mobility of the migrants. All the inhabitants in the camps seem to be on the move, walking on a two-way street between the camps and the tenancies. Women's time is fully occupied by work in the field and at home. Without the help of my counterparts particularly those I have chosen from amongst the women migrants, it would not have been easy to meet all the women who I interviewed. In addition, my gender and research experience made it easier for me to forge links and to build good relationship with the women migrants who accepted me into their everyday life.

4.6.5 Data collection and evaluation

Since the concepts and issues linked to this research on women's social networks are more qualitative, the subjectivity of the respondents is central to the

[14] Sheikh is a village leader who is one of the relatively old men in the village / camp.

research. The qualitative social research techniques are the most appropriate procedure. Hence, the empirical data were collected by using semi-structured interviews, group discussions and observations. The anthropological method of participatory observation was used as well being amongst the migrants and the tenants for quite some time. The semi-structured interviews are the main technique beside the group discussions, and observations. The semi-structured interviews means that the interviewer/(s) should have an interview guide. They are generally used when the research associate has only one time to meet the interviewee. The semi-structured interviews gave the respondents a great opportunity to express themselves and state their views in their own words and to emphasise the issues they considered as their priorities (Bernard 2000: 186).

Corresponding to the qualitative methodology, the evaluation of the empirical data was emphasised, on the one hand, on the individual particularities relevant to the issue under study and, on the other hand, on the grouping of the empirical data into types which express commonalities (Streiffeler and Piszczek 2004: 2). Based on the qualitative methodology, a limited number of actors were interviewed from each ethnic group. Not all interviews were selected for evaluation but in the selected ones most of the respondents came to the point very quickly and provided rich information. It is worth mentioning that, for the sake of keeping my commitment to confidentiality, I do not mention the name of the respondents instead, I have chosen only to describe them by age, ethnic background, social status and form of labour. For the same purpose I have also changed the names of my counterparts and a few respondents whom I choose as case studies in chapter eight.

4.7 A framework for analysis

To derive implications for large networks of relations, it is necessary to frame the basic ways of analysing the empirical research data more precisely. Dey (1993) asserts that an introduction of refined distinctions should be contemplated if we are confident that these distinctions are sufficiently grounded conceptually and empirically to form a useful framework for the analysis (Dey 1993: 105). The strategy of this research, therefore, is to analyse women's social networks by choosing features and aspects of their social interactions in two different spheres. These realms, the work and the private sphere, are used as a constructed methodological instrument, which helps in the analysis of women's social networks.

4.7.1 Work sphere

In general terms, the work sphere means any activity, e.g. social processes, social practices, strategies and social actions related to work. Women migrants' work in the agricultural fields constitutes most of their daily life and their participation in the agricultural work became very substantial. Consequently, the work sphere has been chosen as one of the methodological instruments for the analysis. Forms and formalizations of women' social networks in the work sphere are important incidences to be discussed by the analysis. Women's social networks in the work sphere comprise the analysis of all forms of social networks between women belonging to the ethnic group/ a single 'cohesive subgroup' and between women migrants and other actors involved: women of the local community and the men migrants and men tenants. The analysis covers the ways and dissemination of information diffusion through networking. This way the analysis covers various social interactions and social processes that women migrants experience in the work sphere. The processes of information diffusion about work are analysed in terms of the methods and strategies women apply via their social networks to acquire information about work opportunities and to actually find work opportunities. Consequences of flow of information in maintenance of weak ties will also be highlighted (ref. to Granovetter 1973). Further, social processes of work negotiations in addition to work negotiation power and decision-making process are fundamental issues to be analysed in order to see how women manage to get work opportunities.

The work sphere also presents social networks between the tenants and their partners (sharecroppers) in terms of analysing the factors that lead to continuity and discontinuity of the partnership. It is useful to see what the elements that stabilize social networks between the two partners are, based also on the perception of the tenants and their partners (sharecroppers). The analysis will also be developed further through examining the prevalence of strong or weak ties between the tenants' community and the women migrants. This will assist in determining whether the social networks are strong or fragmented between those two communities and what the factors that lead to maintenance of the weak ties are (ref. to Granovetter, 1973).

Women's strategies are to be explored in terms of discussing how women use their social networks to resolve their problems in their work sphere. The analysis not only depicts the strategies or social practices of women but also develops the analysis further by interpreting why some women groups are able to organize themselves in their networking while others are not. Here I found Granovetter's (1973) inquiry useful by looking into: why some communities organize for common goals quite easily and effectively while others seem to be unable to mobilize resources even against dire threats (Ibid: 1373). Moreover, the analysis does not overlook networking fragmentation particularly if ethnic, cultural or other visible differences do not identify the 'cliques'.

Since women are targeted by the study and considered as a central analytical group, it is necessary to engender the vision of the analysis. Since gender is considered as a social and cultural construction, gender, class and ethnicity are to be considered by the analysis. As noted by Nageeb (2004) class and ethnicity are central factors in breaking down what is meant by gender and how it shapes women's everyday life (Nageeb 2004: 3) comprising women's construction of their social networks. On these bases the issue of gender is an important analytical dimension in the construction of women's work negotiations. To draw the threads together, gender and gender relations as related to work are to be discussed since men are involved in the process of women's work negotiations. Thus, gender relations are considered by this study as a form of social relations that encompasses women and men as actors. Gender relations are to be analysed in the view of 'transitive relations'.

4.7.2 Women's private sphere

Examining the women migrants' everyday life and the construction of their social networks draws attention to the existence of cultural boundaries between women and men's social world. This means that gender produces a different division of the migrants' social world. Thus, the extreme 'gender segregation' that shapes the outlook of the social world of the migrant communities explicates the choice of the women's private sphere as a decisive component in the framework of analysis. It is useful to refer to the following argument of Long (1992) that women are actively engaged in the construction of their own social worlds (Long 1992: 24). Derived from Long's argument women's private sphere is defined in terms of how women construct their social networks in their own world. Therefore, the analysis examines how women migrants belonging to each single 'cohesive subgroup' and to different 'cohesive subgroups' attempt to create a private sphere parallel to that of men. It is also useful here to refer to Nageeb's (2004) definition of women's private space as a commitment to the cultural system, which is expressed in women's construction of their social world and of social, physical and domestic reproduction. She went further in clarifying the meaning of private space by looking into women's social practices, such as women gatherings as spaces for social networking (Nageeb 2004: 44). However, women's practices, such as informal social associations and the other different forms of mutual social support which women render and women's gatherings, are considered by this study as women's activities and strategies which they apply by means of their social networks.

Inter-household relations: a women's private sphere

Women's private sphere does not simply indicate that the concept of private is only associated with the household as regards the activities and social contacts of women within the household. Thus, it is important to understand that the women's private sphere underlines in addition to other activities the ones that women carry out in the context of inter-household relations. The inter-household relations include traditional relations that combine the women migrants in their 'cliques', such as ethnic, kin and neighbourhood. The constitution of household as women's private sphere according to Schultz (2005) does not signify that women's activities are confined to domestic work and family contacts. The household in Sudan has a public character. The house is the focal point of social networking among relatives and neighbours. It is a component of the women's public sphere, in which women cultivate social contacts that also have an economic significance for their families. The social relationships between the women are not only economically important but also cultivate a status system independent of men, reflected in their position in the family (Schultz 2005: 143). However, it is important to stress at this stage that on the one hand, since the focus of this study is social networks among groups of the women migrants, the inter-household relations and not the household relations or family relations are an important analytical component. On the other hand, in the social context of the migrant communities in the Gezira Scheme, there tends to be a clear dichotomy between the social worlds of two gender categories (women and men). This is attributed to the migrants' social realities that generate a tendency towards gender separatism which shapes the outlook of the migrants' social world. Consequently, this fosters women as actors to construct social networks in a social world of their own even in a realm, which is supposed to encompass women and men. Nageeb's (2004) following argument in her writing about the women's private space suits this situation. Women's private space enables women to practice their social power in controlling their space by eliminating the presence of others whose presence would shift the definition of private space to a public one (Nageeb 2004: 186).

This way, women's multiple realities and diverse mutual social support and strategies can be recognized and comparison of women's different and incompatible social worlds can be grasped.

Notes

(1) Definitions of social isolation in Web:
A feeling of aloneness experienced by the individual as a threatening state imposed by others; a sense of aloneness caused by the absence of family and friends; the absence of a supportive or significant personal relationship caused by the patient's unacceptable social behaviour or social values, the inability to engage in social situations, immature interests, inappropriate attitudes for the developmental age of the individual, alterations in physical appearance, or mental status or illness. www.birf.info/home/bi-tools/qlinks_s.html Definition im Kontext.

5. Work sphere: getting work opportunities

5.1 An introduction

Examining the pillars of the social structure predominant in the Gezira Scheme, one notices that it is the migrants who are doing the hard work in the fields. As to women, sociological research has shown that women's involvement in the agricultural labour force is substantial. As pointed out by Yousif (1992), the likelihood for women migrants in Gezira to work is high, by national as well as international standards (Yousif, 1992: 86–87). Due to the availability of many groups of women who migrated with their families and settled in the Gezira area and due to the change of women's status from one of seclusion to one of substantial participation in the agricultural labour, women spend almost their entire day in the fields. This indicates that the cultural boundaries between work sphere and home sphere have been removed and the way has been paved for women to leave their homes and go to work. This signifies a noticeable social change and creates a new domain of social networks for women.

The study shows that, women migrants' experiences of their everyday life as well as their social interactions and structures are largely determined by a complex situation. This complexity can be described as women being relocated, thus bringing the cultural background of their societies of origin to a new social world within the Sudan Gezira Scheme, and being engaged in a new form of economic activity alien to the traditional subsistence agriculture in their home of origin. Their social position necessitates analysis of how these women cope in the new location in which they are experiencing this new working atmosphere. On these grounds the study focuses on the methods and strategies women apply to acquire information about work opportunities, actually find work opportunities and undertake work negotiations, which includes a variety of social processes. Furthermore, the analysis underlines the work relations with special emphasis on the conditions under which the partnership — mainly sharecropping — continues or discontinues on the grounds of the empirical research respondents' perception.

5.2 Information diffusion

It is empirically evident that 70 % of the women respondents have been influenced by their male relatives concerning the availability of work opportunities, particularly sharecropping and land sub-leasing in the Gezira area before their migration. Those are particularly women who migrated from Chad where they got hold of information about work opportunities available in the Gezira Scheme. They have access to such information from male relatives who have returned after preceding them in migrating to the Gezira area. Most of the men migrants from Chad return back home to accompany their female relatives in their migration to the Gezira area.

15 % of the women respondents acquired information regarding the availability of work opportunities on sharecropping and land sub-leasing in the Gezira Scheme through their being in the Scheme during the cotton-picking season. Those are Misairia women who migrated from Kordofan Northern State in the West of Sudan and settled in the Gezira Scheme. Before settling in the Scheme they used to work as seasonal workers picking cotton during the off-season of their subsistence traditional agriculture. After settling in the Gezira area women migrants usually acquire information regarding work opportunities through traditional channels and their informal social contacts. These operate either through random communication or through direct or indirect channels. Random communication here means that the respective information is accidentally circulated between women. The likelihood for this to happen is in particular when women meet, either during their gatherings or through their traditional relations. Direct communication means face-to-face communication. It takes place when women communicate with the men tenants without the need of intermediary contacts. Indirect channels signify that the information is transferred through 'transitive relations' where the presence of intermediary contacts is a necessity. These processes of information diffusion are correlated with the forms of labour women are concerned with, which are wage labour, sharecropping and land sub-leasing. It is worth mentioning that women migrants' wage labour covers picking cotton, harvesting vegetables and picking groundnuts. Owing to this correlation, the explanation of information diffusion is based on the ways of communication and the forms of women's labour.

5.2.1 Random and direct channels of communication

Women who belong to the same ethnic group have different ways of connected interactions in different events and activities, in the work sphere as well as in their private sphere. 60 % of the women respondents get information about the need for cotton pickers through their direct contacts with the tenants of whom women are either partners or non-partners. The latter are women who are neither involved in sharecropping nor in land sub-leasing but in cotton picking only. When meeting within their work sphere women transfer the information about wage work to each other through random communication. An example for such information is who among the tenants is in need of cotton pickers from among the women migrants, because there are some tenants who hire women from the poor families of the local community to pick their cotton.

In turn, women in their private sphere announce the need for wage labour randomly during their gatherings or they circulate the respective information through their traditional relations, such as neighbourhood relations as well as kin and in-law relations. It is noteworthy that, regarding the acquisition of information on the demand for wage labour, almost all women sharecroppers within a single 'cohesive subgroup' give priority to women of the same ethnic group followed by other women who belong to other ethnic groups. In spite of the commonalities in the ways of information acquisition about cotton picking I came across some special cases during the research. A woman from Fellata, aged 38, who works as a cotton picker explains that she transfers information regarding the need of cotton pickers to women of different ethnic groups:

"I work in the field only in cotton picking because I also have other work to do in the houses of the Arabs (1). *There is a tenant in this village whom I have known for quite long time, his name is Taha. He used to come to me every cotton-picking season and ask me to collect women to pick his cotton. He also gives me the money to distribute to those women according to price of the Goffa. So, first I tell my neighbours. One is from 'Kardafa' and another one is from Hausa - and then, after that I tell all the other women who could pick cotton until I gather enough workers."*

The particularity of this woman from Fellata offering the information about the need for cotton pickers to women of different ethnic groups might be attributed to the fact that Fellata women do not usually work in cotton picking. This woman is in fact the only woman from Fellata that works as a cotton picker, at least in the localities this study focuses on. Furthermore, she combines her work in cotton picking with tertiary work in the houses of the people of the local community.

Another particular case shows that four women respondents, who work as sharecroppers and live at the periphery of one of the two villages this study focuses on, make sure that one way they get hold of information about cotton picking is through a wife of a tenant living in the village. Tracing the information back to its source this study found that this woman is a migrant from Fellata whose husband is also from Fellata who inherited the tenancy from his father. Another unique case I came across during the empirical research is in the locality that is inhabited by a diversity of ethnic groups. A man tenant who stays among the migrants in Daim[15] Wad Ellaithie has built strong ties with the migrant communities in this settlement compared to the relations of the tenants' community in the nearby villages with the migrants. Due to the assimilation of this tenant into the migrant community in Daim Wad Ellaithie he acts, during the cotton-picking season, as a contact person between the men tenants who stay in the nearby villages and some of the women migrants in the Daim. He transfers the information about the tenant's need for cotton pickers to these women. They, in turn, who precede their acquaintances in acquiring the information about work opportunities for cotton pickers transfer the message to other women through their traditional relations or when meeting in their private sphere. Again, women give priority regarding the acquisition of information about available wage work opportunities to women of the same ethnic background.

It has been found that 30 % of the women respondents also find out about vegetables harvest through their direct contacts with the men migrants who belong to a single cohesive subgroup. 30 % of the women respondents ensure that they acquire information about the need of labour of groundnuts picking from women and men migrants who work as sharecroppers or land sub-leasers. They get hold of such information through random communication between women and direct contacts with the men migrants. It is noteworthy that these crops (vegetables and groundnuts) are included in the sharecropping and land sub-leasing. The vegetable production is recognised as men's work whereas women carry out the har-

[15] There is a tenant's family whose grandfather is the one who established Daim Wad Ellaithie — which is named after him Wad Ellaithie — for the settlement of the migrants who used to work in his tenancies as seasonal labourers, who later on came to work as partners either in his tenancies or in other tenancies. Several ethnic groups joined these migrants and settled in this compound (settlement). This family of Wad Ellaithie has kept their grandfather's tradition of living among the migrants (at the periphery of the Daim). Daim, as this man and some other people who stay there explained to me, is a big camp. According on my observations it is also quite a big camp compared to other existing camps and without social services other than a big water pipe, which is locally called *'Kargaka'* and is used by all the Daim settlers.

vest. It is important to note here that 60 % of the women respondents assure that they carry out the harvest particularly of groundnuts and sorghum through 'Nafeer' a form of mutual collective work, which is explained in the next chapter.

5.2.2 Indirect channels of communication

With the exception of the women respondents from Beni Halba the majority (more than 75 %) of the women respondents assured that after their settlement in the Gezira area they find out about the work opportunities with their partners in sharecropping and land sub-leasing through their men relatives, i.e. through indirect channels of communication. In their search for work opportunities for women men migrants obtain the necessary information either through asking their contacts among the men tenants about work opportunities or, as pointed out by Scott (1991), they acquire information accidentally whenever contacts (men tenants) volunteer the information (Scott 1991:35). It is remarkable that the women respondents neither expect to get hold of the information about work opportunities on sharecropping or land sub-leasing through women contacts with the men tenants nor through women within or outside the same ethnic group. However, despite the commonalities there is discrepancy between the norm and practice, as the following particular cases will show.

A married woman from Bargo, aged 24, who is a sharecropper said:
"My aunt has been a partner of our current sharecropper for 9 years and she told us about his need for more sharecroppers. She introduced us to him and we became his partners. My aunt still works with him."
A woman from Beni Halba at the age of 47 who also works as a sharecropper mentioned that:
"Last year, I heard from my old partner that he needed people to work with him as sharecroppers. I promised him that I would tell two of my female relatives who I knew would like to work as sharecroppers. I then told my relatives, who agreed to work for him".

It has also been realised that only about 15 % of the women respondents, who are mostly not married, get information on sharecropping through their social networks with women of the local community who are not engaged in the agricultural work. Those women migrants belong to a group of Bargo who used to stay for a long time within a village of the local community and, recently, this group has evacuated the village due to a request from the villagers (i.e. people of the local community) (2). These unmarried women migrants who were born in that village were able to build social relations with a few women of their age from the local community before their respective group left the village. A young unmarried woman respondent aged 22, from Bargo found out about a new work opportunity in sharecropping outside the 'cohesive subgroup' to which she belongs. She acquired the information through her personal contact with some unmarried women who are daughters of a tenant and with whom she could build a social relation. Through this woman respondent this information reached her sister who is socially distant (3) from women of the local community. This is the way this Bargo woman describes how the information process takes place:

"I heard about my partner and his need for a sharecropper from his daughters whom I got to know while we were staying in the village. I used to visit them sometimes. They told their father about me and he agreed. I told my elder sister then and discussed the issue with her and she also agreed. This is the way we became his partners it."

It is remarkable that there is a very little search for work opportunities on sharecropping and land sub-leasing through connections of women migrants with women tenants as compared to their contacts with the men tenants. This is because women migrants' have lesser contacts with the women tenants than they have with the men tenants who are the majority. This is attributable to the fact that the men tenants represent the majority while the women tenants are few in number as they acquire only 12 % of the tenancies in the whole Scheme.
Only four women among the total number of the women respondents are partners of women tenants. An example of a sharecropper at the age of 48 from Beni Halba who stays in Wad Ellaithie and whose partner is a woman tenant explains the way through which she procured the information about her current partner:

"A woman from 'Kardafa' (Misairia) with whom I have a good relation told me about the need of a woman tenant for a sharecropper. She introduced me to her because she used to be her old partner".

5.2.3 Information diffusion across boarders

Interpersonal ties with their men relatives link the women before their migration with the former men migrants through the bonds of kin and shared community of origin. The decision to migrate and how to cope in the Gezira area as a new location are greatly influenced by ethnic and kinship networks in which people are involved (Morawska 1990 and Massey 1988 in Powell and Smith-Doerr 1994:374). The reasons that drive women to migrate are influenced by the knowledge about work opportunities they are able to gain in advance. These are considered as strong pull factors that encouraged women to migrate and they are increasingly independent of the conditions that generated immigration in the first place (ref. to Powell and Smith-Doerr 1994:374). These conditions are draught and desertification, poverty and conflicts. One could argue that social networks influence women's migration and work. As a consequence of the manner the respective information is distributed women migrants' participation in the labour force of the Gezira Scheme has increased substantially. The process of information distribution described above also shows the interlocking of the migrants with the ones they left behind and their social cohesion across boarders.

5.2.4 Which forms of women's labour? Which channels of communication?

The process of information flow to women migrants in the Gezira Scheme is a complex process involving various actor yet analytically separable channels of information diffusion. Social networks facilitate the process of distributing information about women's work opportunities but the functions served by the networks vary with the forms of women's labour. These forms also correlate with specific channels of information flow. Wage work is correlated with random communication and direct channels of communication. Women who belong to a single 'cohesive subgroup' have access to the information about wage labour either through their direct contacts with the men tenants and men migrants or through random communication among themselves. (See figure 3) Sharecropping and land sub-leasing are correlated with indirect channels of communication. Indirect channels have been found through male relatives or women of the local community who act as intermediary contacts between the men tenants and the women migrants. (See figure 4) They provide the women migrants with new information about work opportunities on sharecropping and land subleasing that they would not likely receive within their own immediate social networks.

5.2.5 Wage work: a correlation with random communication and direct channels

Women migrants get hold of information about wage work through random communication among the women themselves and through their direct contacts with the men migrants as well as the men tenants. (See figure 3) Since vegetable production is men migrants' work and the vegetable harvest is women's work, women acquire information on the need of wageworkers for vegetable harvest within the cohesive subgroup. Women get hold of such information within a 'cohesive subgroup' either through direct channels of communication with the men migrants or through their random communication with each other. As to groundnuts picking, women usually carry it out. With the exception of Bargo and Tama who pick their groundnuts through *'Nafeer'*, other existing ethnic groups pick their groundnuts through wage work. In case wageworkers are needed for groundnuts picking women acquire such information through their random communication with each other. This is because groundnuts are one of the crops that are grown under sharecropping and land sub-leasing. This means that it is either produced by women only or by women and their male relatives. This facilitates the process of distribution of information about the groundnuts picking among women. (See figure 3).

Figure 3: Information diffusion on wage work: direct and random channels of communication

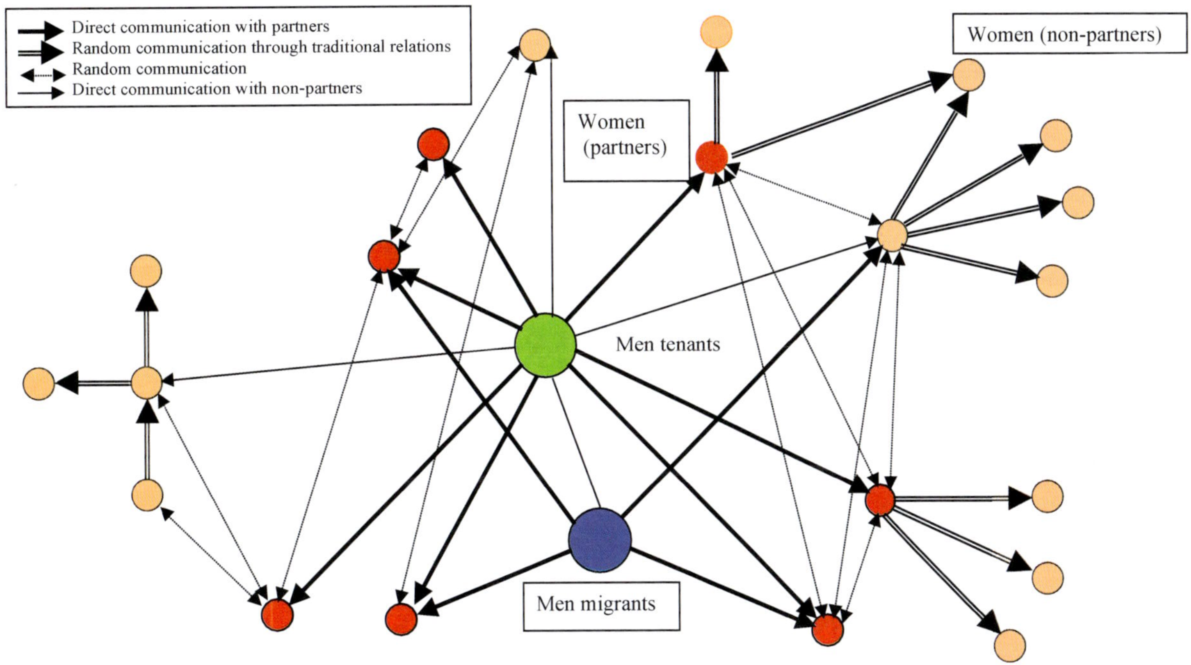

Differing from the situation women are in when involved in processes of transitive relations (i.e. indirect channels of communication) women do not need intermediary contacts to get hold of information about the wage work from the men tenants. This is attributable to the fact that the wage work is a group work, and being in groups women are permitted by their traditional and cultural discourses to discuss the wages with the tenants whenever there is a need to do that. As far as cotton picking is concerned it has to be noted that the Sudan Gezira Board (SGB) seasonally determines the price of *'Goffa'*, which means that women do not negotiate the price of cotton picking with the tenants. According to the Gezira Scheme Tenancy Agreement of 1927, however, the tenants are responsible for recruiting the people needed for wage labour. This implies that each tenant needs to choose which group he encounters to pick her/his cotton. This fact necessitates direct contacts of the tenants with the cotton pickers. Since cotton picking is women's work, they do in fact work in groups moving from one tenancy to another. This way of working in groups facilitates on the one hand the direct communication between different groups of cotton pickers (women) and the tenants. On the other hand it also facilitates the distribution of information among women through their random communication with each other.

As to information diffusion about wage work among women, there are conditions that facilitate this process. Since women within a single 'cohesive subgroup' have many 'overlapping' contacts and relations with one another, they all tend to know and interact with each other in numerous situations. Therefore there is a tendency for them to possess the same knowledge about work opportunities particularly on wage labour (ref. to Granovetter 1974:54), which they transfer among themselves through random communication. Women transfer the information about wage work through their 'cliques', traditional relations (e.g. neighbourhood and kin relations), and meetings at activities and events. Women's gatherings in their private sphere like gatherings for coffee or a group visit if one of them is sick or has given birth, also facilitate the circulation of such information. It has been found out that through women's meetings at events and activities, a linkage between these events and activities is established. This is because the same group of women within a single 'cohesive subgroup' participates in the same activities, which is often referred to as 'overlapping of relations'. Hence, 'overlapping' of relations between women of the same ethnic group is significant. Such 'overlapping' of women's relations as results from women's interactions in different events and activities allows for random com-

munication and hence for the flow of information between women about the wage work. Thus, as pointed out by Granovetter (1973), the information flows more easily due to the speciality, giving it some *"sense of community,"* activated at meetings and conventions (Granovetter 1973:1373).
Involvement of women in the process of information diffusion on wage work to their acquaintances and giving priority of access to such information to women of the co-ethnic group is evident. This expresses on the one hand the feeling of 'intimacy' and coherence and the bond of 'belonging' to one ethnic group, which demonstrates the availability of what Macharia (1988) calls "ethnic biases." (Macharia 1988:15) Since the ethnic biases are evident in the allocation of available work opportunities in the wage labour to co-ethnics it is clear that ethnic identity matters greatly to women migrants. On the other hand this form of interconnectedness smoothes the progress of building new relations and generating work opportunities in the coming seasons for women who are newly engaged in the wage work.
From what has been explained it is evident that the wage work is correlated with two means of information diffusion: random communication and direct channels.

5.2.6 Sharecropping and land subleasing: a correlation
5.2.6 with indirect channels

To explain the findings on the social process of information dissemination on sharecropping and land sub-leasing through indirect channels, application of Granovetter's (1974) information diffusion model is found to be useful. This can be explained, if one looks into the process of information transfer through the transitive relations where men migrants act as intermediaries. Men tenants with work information pass them on to a certain proportion of the men migrants who are considered as their immediate contacts who, in turn, pass them on to a certain number of their contacts who are women migrants. (See figure 4) Furthermore, it is possible to trace the information through women's social networks so as to know who acquires the information and their various locations in the network. Therefore, the acquisition of information depends firstly upon the motivation of those who have information and are free to pass it on. Men tenants get the benefit of the partnership, men migrants either supplement the households' income or, in other cases where women are head of the household, they assist them in generating income for their respective households, and women migrants guarantee continuity of their partnership; and secondly it depends on the strategic location of people's contacts in the flow of information (ref. to Granovetter 1974:52).

Men tenants are central in the network since they possess the information about work opportunities. Their 'centrality' emanates from their control of the tenancies (i.e. 'land centrality') that gives them 'power' to decide which information to pass on and to whom. Men migrants are also central; however, they are less central than the men tenants. Their 'centrality' relies on their information acquisition from the tenants as well as their intermediate position in the network. Thus, men migrants' 'centrality' implies their strategic location in women migrants' networks. This strategic location is attributable to the available traditional and cultural discourse of the migrants, which abandon the women migrants' direct contacts with the men tenants, particularly those tenants with whom the women migrants have never worked in sharecropping or land subleasing before. Unlike the wage work sharecropping and land sub-leasing require the tenant to get in contact with the person he passes the information about his need of a sharecropper or a land sub-leaser to. The men tenants are aware of the migrants' cultural discourse, which does not permit them to have personal contacts with most of the women migrants, particularly those with whom the tenants are not engaged in sharecropping and/or land sub-leasing. Within this cultural discourse the greater part of the women migrants' contacts with the men tenants is restricted by involvement of the men migrants. Thus, the men migrants' personal contacts with the men tenants are primary channels of search for work and the information transfer on sharecropping and land sub-leasing to women migrants. (See figure 4) This applies in particular to Bargo and Tama women and a large proportion from Fellata, Hausa and Misairia.

The analysis lays special emphasis on the nature of the ties between men tenants and men migrants, since the latter act as intermediary contacts in the transfer of information about sharecropping and land sub-leasing to the majority of the women migrants. Women's access to information about sharecropping and land sub-leasing became feasible through men migrants. This feasibility is attributed to the easiness of contact between the men because of their gender and to the engagement of the men migrants in their work with the men tenants for a long period of time. These facts make their interaction with the men tenants most intense and most regular, i.e. they provide for an 'effective network', which manifests itself in strong ties between them. This is strong evidence for Granovetter's argument that says: Most mutual choices indicate strong ties and the configuration of strong ties became increasingly frequent, as people knew one another longer and better (Granovetter 1973:1364). Hence, a significant finding is that women acquire agency since they take advantage of men migrants' strong ties with the men tenants and of the accessibility of information about sharecropping and land sub-leasing through the men migrants. The tenants, for their part, put emphasis on the reliability on their new work partners (sharecroppers and/or land sub-leasers). One way to guarantee reliability and continuity of the work relations is the transfer of the information (about work opportunities in sharecropping and land sub-leasing) to the men migrants with whom the men tenants have social contacts or with whom they have worked before. This is mainly with the intention of establishing their new partnership through people whom they trust and whom they have already seen to be reliable. Likewise, Granovetter (1985) suggests that we trust best those informants we have dealt with in the past and have found to be reliable (Granovetter 1985).

It is therefore through the men migrants in different work situations and through their wide social horizons with the men tenants that new information about work opportunities on sharecropping and land sub-leasing is most likely become available to the women migrants. Conversely, women migrants are less likely to be the sources of new information about sharecropping and land sub-leasing from more distant parts of the networks, e.g. the men tenants. This implies the existence of 'gender segregation' between the majority of the women migrants and the men tenants, for which the cultural and traditional discourses of the migrants' communities are held responsible. These discourses limit the women migrants' contacts with the men outside their ethnic groups. This interprets that gender and ethnic identity are primary factors in constructing the channels of communication between these women and the men tenants.

It has been found that women of the local community are new actors in transmitting information between the tenants and the women migrants. One should note that most women of the local community are not engaged in the agricultural labour force. However, their being part of the tenants' community has given them the right to have access to information about work opportunities, e.g. sharecropping, which they randomly transfer to the women migrants with whom they have some sort of contact. This way, women of the local community are considered to be intermediary contacts between the women migrants and the men tenants in the process of transferring information on sharecropping and land subleasing. Unmarried women migrants, on the other hand, manipulate their social networks with the women of the local community in their attempt to receive information about work opportunities, particularly in sharecropping. This way, unmarried women migrants make use of their social networks with the women of the local community as well as of the position of these women are in with regard to the fact that they are members of the tenants' community. The women migrants use these circumstances by using 'transitive logic', i.e. indirect channels, and consequently they could preserve the traditional and cultural discourses of their societies.

Figure 4: Information diffusion on sharecropping and land subleasing: indirect channels

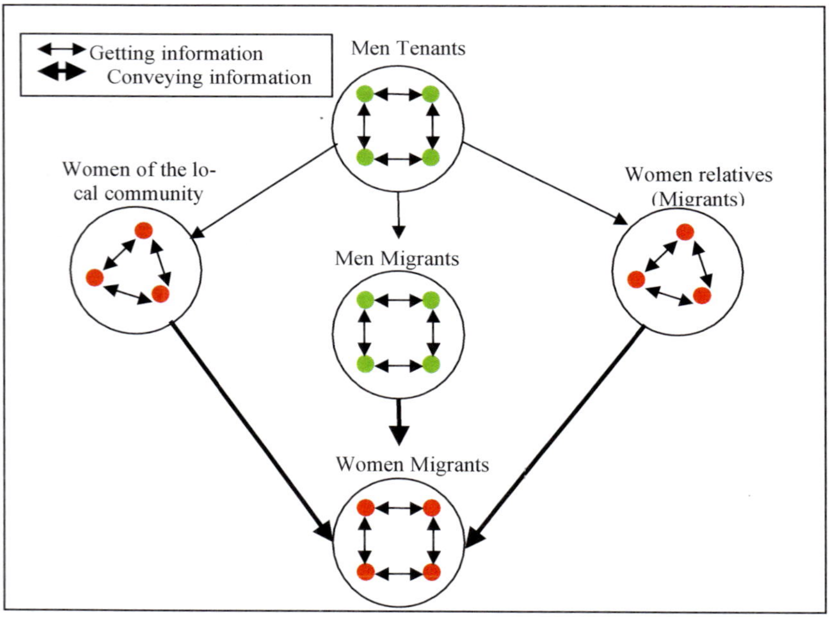

5.2.7 'Transitivity': a compelling force in the social process of information diffusion

Since the dissemination of information on sharecropping and land sub-leasing is enabled by the use of indirect channels, 'transitivity' is considered to be a compelling force in the social process of information diffusion. 'Transitivity' made it possible for women to acquire high mobility within the work sphere. It also maintains their local ties with the men migrants within the 'cohesive subgroup' they belong to and with women of the local community they have some form of social contact with. Based on this of analysis that emphasises the 'logic of transitivity', I agree with Granovetter's (1973) point of view that the weak ties are an important resource in providing for a higher level of mobility and that they also play a role in affecting social cohesion (Granovetter 1973:1373). Granovetter's theory of weak ties is proven in the context of rural Sudan through the existence of transitive relations. The weak ties here do not only result in women's acquisition of information on sharecropping and land sub-leasing and in enabling women to be mobile within the work sphere. They also maintain the social cohesion between the women and men migrants of the same ethnic group and between the women migrants and the women of the local community the women migrants have social contact with. Unlike wage work, acquiring information on sharecropping and land sub-leasing requires personal contact to get detailed information. This information can be represented in how many feddan the tenant would like to share or sub-lease, which crop he wants the sharecropper to grow, and for how many years. Despite the fact that women migrants are conditioned by the traditional and cultural discourses of their societies, which control their social interactions with men outside their ethnic group, they demonstrate that they are themselves social actors. This is manifest in finding their way to get hold of information on sharecropping and land sub-leasing through transitive relations. They acquire agency and 'power' by using the social relations between the men migrants and men tenants and by manipulating their social networks with the women of the local community to get hold of information. (This kind of women's 'power' is explained more clearly later in this chapter.) The way women construct their social networks and their ability to take advantage of the given circumstances is a significant finding that consolidates the idea of the actor-oriented approach.

5.3 Undertaking work negotiations

"It is taboo and shameful for us, just like you."

It is empirically evident in all cases, with the exception of most of the respondents from Beni Halba, that married as well as unmarried women respondents do not undertake work negotiations on sharecropping or land sub-leasing with the men tenants themselves. Moreover, compared to married women, unmarried women are even further restricted in undertaking work negotiations. This is the way an unmarried woman from Bargo describes undertaking their work negotiations with the men tenants:

"It is taboo and shameful for us, just like you (she means the women of the local community). *You cannot stay with a strange person, only if she is a woman but not with men. We women cannot ask men to rent their lands to us. But if the lady is married she can talk to the tenant with whom she is sharing crop or from whom she is renting land. [...] And this happens rarely, like in case of the need to transfer what the tenant would like to say to her man (i.e. husband). This happens only in case of the absence of our men in the field [...]. But it is a big taboo for the unmarried woman to do so. For example, I never met the man from whom I rented the tenancy for five years and I never discussed the tenancy business with him, as my uncle is the one who undertakes these issues."*

With the vast majority (80 %) of the women respondents the negotiations for women's work in sharecropping or land sub-leasing rest with male relatives of the women such as husbands, brothers, fathers or brothers in-law. If the husband or the other men of the family are absent the responsibility goes instantly to the men in the neighbourhood, the *'sheikh'*, men relatives or even other men from the same ethnic group, who act as intermediaries between the women and men tenants. This is common among Bargo and Tama, of whom women do not have contacts with the men tenants throughout the partnership and do not even attend the work negotiations. This implies that Bargo and Tama women and men tenants are 'nonadjacent actors'. However, in some cases, work agreements are based on women's consensus.

A 30-year-old married woman from Tama who works as a sharecropper expressed her views on who undertakes the work negotiations with the tenants as follows:

"The man always goes ahead of the woman. Whenever there is any man from the tribe he speaks on behalf of the woman. These are our customs. It will never happen that a woman goes ahead of the man because this is a big mistake and a taboo".

Unlike in the case of Bargo and Tama, another form of 'transitivity' exists where there is a direct contact between women and men tenants. This is found in the case of all women respondents who work as sharecroppers and land sub-leasers from Misairia, Fellata and Hausa where women participate in the work negotiations and give their consensus in the work deal. However, company of the husband is a pre-requisite for the presence of a woman when the work negotiations with the men tenants on the sharecropping or land sub-leasing take place.

Between the Bargo women and the men tenants, however, another form of 'transitivity' is established through women of the local community. Some of these are new actors in women's work negotiations who act as intermediaries between Bargo women and men tenants. A few women respondents (15 %) were able to build social relations with wives and daughters of the tenants using which these women migrants get work opportunities from the men tenants.

A young unmarried woman, aged 19, from Bargo expressed the way through which she acquired the information about work and how she became a sharecropper:

"It is shameful for us to discuss business issues with the men tenants. With regard to my sharecropper, I did not discuss the issue myself but through his daughters whom I have known since we were living in the 'Arab's' village and with whom I chat. When I explained to them that I was in need of work, they told me that their father was looking for a sharecropper and would help me by sharing his tenancy with me if I grew groundnuts. ... And finally the agreement was made through the tenant's daughters."

Another form of connection between women migrants and men tenants is established through women migrants who work as sharecroppers. This is manifest where some of the tenants rely on their women sharecroppers to either carry out all the agricultural operations concerning the cotton or at least carry out the cotton picking (4). Since cotton picking is regarded as women's work, most of the women respondents from Misairia and Beni Halba, Fellata and Hausa (80 %) assist their partners (tenants) in shouldering the responsibility for recruiting other cotton pickers and distributing their wages. Almost all women sharecroppers (more than 95 % of them) usually give the priority of wage labour to women who belong to their ethnic group who move as a group from one tenancy to another in order to pick the cotton. One should note here that the majority (about 75 %) of the Bargo and Tama women respondents assured that they do not participate in the process of cotton picking because it coincides with the harvest time of the groundnuts.

As to Beni Halba women, 80 % of the women respondents from this ethnic group assured that they search for work and undertake work negotiations on sharecropping and land sub-leasing through their direct contact with the men tenants. Those are either married or divorced women, whereas the unmarried women rely either on their mothers or their fathers in undertaking the work negotiations. A divorced woman from Beni Halba, aged 47, who works as a sharecropper as well as a wage labourer explains the way she undertakes the work negotiations and how the women of Beni Halba interact with the men tenants:

"I got to know my partner by myself. The tenant came to us here and told us about the work. I talked to him myself and then we agreed on the partnership. In the case of cotton picking, the tenant comes to our houses and asks us to work with him. He tells us (the women) about the price of the 'Goffa'. We talk to the tenant about the sharecropping and the price of cotton picking but no, I couldn't work with a foreign tenant alone except in a group with other women".

Another woman from Beni Halba, divorced, aged 50, and works as a sharecropper as well as a wage labourer explains how did she get to know her partners and the way she undertakes the work negotiations:

" I am a partner of two tenants. One is a man. Yes, I talked to him myself when I wanted to become his partner. I had known him for long time. I am also a partner of a woman tenant. I know a woman here in Wad Ellaithie from 'Kardafa' (Misairia). *I have a good relationship with her... She and her daughters are very kind to me. She introduced me to Nagat (a woman tenant) with whom she shares crop. She knew that Nagat was looking for someone with whom to share crop. Then I talked to this woman* (the tenant) *and we became partners".*

In a focus group discussion of which participants are unmarried women from the different ethnic groups in Wad Ellaithie, an unmarried woman from Beni Halba says:

"The girls do not discuss work issues with the tenants but our mothers and our fathers do and we work with them. Some of us work in sharecropping and the others work in 'Eldangada'. We all do wage work such as cotton picking, too".

5.3.1 Discussion

It is crucial at the outset of the analysis of women's work negotiations to note that in sharecropping and land sub-leasing negotiations need to be undertaken and the respective work deal needs to be agreed upon with single persons. Unlike sharecropping and land sub-leasing, in wage work such as cotton picking, groundnuts picking, and vegetable harvest, there are no negotiations to be undertaken or work deals to be agreed upon between the tenants or men migrants and the agricultural labourers who are exclusively women. In the case of cotton picking this is attributable to the fact that the Sudan Gezira Board (SGB) determines the price of cotton picking annually. However, tenants who belong to the same field inspection office (5) may make minor changes in the price of the *'Goffa'* determined by the SGB. Nevertheless, the new price is also fixed and agreed upon by all tenants concerned. Since the price of cotton picking is fixed there are no work negotiations as such that take place between the women who work as cotton pickers and the tenants. In case of groundnuts picking and vegetable harvest the price that is one third of the harvesting amount is also fixed and agreed upon among the migrants' communities. This means that the analysis accentuates the work negotiations in terms of sharecropping and land sub-leasing. However, cotton picking appears in the analysis where women sharecroppers are engaged in the processes of cotton picking and collection of the cotton pickers.

The study has found that the work negotiations take place between the different kinds of actors. These actors include men migrants, women migrants, women of the local community and the men tenants and all of these actors have specific positions and interact differently within the network. (See figure 5) Hence, the focus of the analysis is on: 1/ the position of the different kinds of actors in the women's networks, 2/ the way the women migrants interact with these actors socially in order to participate in their work negotiations and, 3/ the different ways these actors employ to undertake the work negotiations. On these grounds the analysis underlines the different ways of undertaking the women's work negotiations within the social context of the Gezira Scheme, which includes the ethnically heterogeneous groups of the migrants and the people of the local community. (See figure 5)

Figure 5: Undertaking women's work negotiations: sharecropping and land subleasing

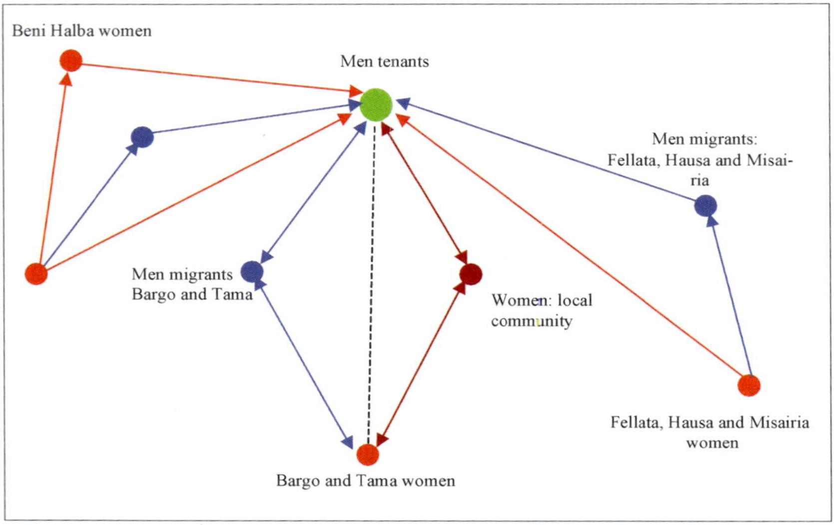

5.3.2 Men's intermediation in transitive relations

Men migrants' involvement in women's work negotiations, whether the women concerned are active participants in these negotiations or not, signifies that men are central in women's social networks. Men migrants' prominence and importance in women's networks emanate from their wide social horizons and extensive relationship with the men tenants plus the existence of the traditional and cultural discourses of the migrants' original societies that control women's social interactions with the men tenants. Consequently, this cultural discourse is held responsible for keeping most of the women segregated from all men not belonging to their ethnic groups. Therefore the relationship between women migrants and the men tenants is transitive which reflects an aspect of 'centrality'.

To gain a better understanding about how important these actors (the men migrants in particular) are as intermediaries it is significant to note that some of them have some 'interpersonal influence' on the other actors (women migrants and men tenants). This explains their importance in the network, as they are not only a means of 'interconnectedness' between the other actors. Similarly Wasserman and Faust (1994) conceptualise the importance of the actors in the middle as 'betweeness centrality'. This is because the interactions between the two 'non-adjacent actors' might particularly depend on the actors who are in the middle. Those actors potentially might have some control over the interactions between the two non-adjacent actors (Wasserman and Faust 1994:188). This is particularly true in a few cases of Bargo and Tama where there is influence of some men who fully control the work negotiations. This is due to the fact that these men work mainly as sharecroppers or land sub-leasers as do their wives. Since these men are partners, one can contend that they may also have some influence on the continuity of (their and their wives') partnership with the men tenants. Their 'betweeness centrality' in the network may lead in some cases to discontinuity of the partnership. On the other hand men tenants are also central in the partnership due to the fact that the tenancies are under their control, i.e. 'centrality of land'. One could argue at this point that the 'power' they acquire from this 'centrality' can in some cases lead to conflicts with the men migrants. Consequently, such conflicts may ultimately lead to termination of the partnership, since selling of the agricultural labour force in the Gezira Scheme is a process of 'free labour formation' (6). Wassermann and Faust (1994) assert that: *"Truly central actors will force many discontinued components to arise"* (ibid: 218). Hence, the above discussion demonstrates a correlation between 'centrality' and 'power' within inter-groups' networks. It also shows how distinctive actors across 'centrality' are.

Nevertheless, women should not be considered as passive, since they certainly are active actors within the networks. Though men are central in women's social networks women gain 'power' too, through the construction of these social networks. "*Women's power lies in their relationships, where they use personal connections and influence to gain power*" contends White (1992), (White 1992:186 in Smith 1994:557). The women's 'power' that lies in their relationships can be explained here where women use their men relatives' wide social horizons and social networks with the men tenants to get hold of information and to get work opportunities. Consequently, women penetrate the tenants' work and work relations to achieve their goals in everyday life whilst maintaining their economic and social identity as women's labour. This way, they also preserve the cultural and social discourses of their societies in which they experience their everyday life and construct their social networks. Hence, social networks as White (1992) defines them are *"a source of women's power"* (ibid: 558). This kind of power can further be explained by looking at the case of Bargo and Tama women who do not usually participate in the work negotiations although some of them might possibly influence the negotiations. A widow from Tama, aged 55, asserts the following:

"I am sharing the tenant who was a partner of my late husband. I asked my elder son, who first approached him, to tell him that I would need to share two feddan with him, in one of which my daughter and I would cultivate groundnuts and, in the other, sorghum. I told my son not to accept whatever the tenant would say to him (i.e. any offer) *without my consent."*

Hence, the different patterns of social organisation that emerge result from the interactions, negotiations, and social struggles that take place between the different kinds of actors. These actors include not only those present in any given face-to-face encounter but also those who are absent but have nonetheless influence on the situation, the actions and the outcomes (Long 2001:13). Furthermore, the ability to influence others or to pass on a command rests fundamentally on *"the actions of a chain of agents each of whom translates it in accordance with her or his own projects"* and power is composed here by enrolling other actors in a given social scheme (Latour 1986:264 in Long 2001:17 and Long 2001:17). In other words, agency and power are essentially dependent upon the emergence of a network of actors who become partially, though hardly ever completely, enrolled in the 'project' of some other person or persons (Long 2001:17). To conclude, one should emphasise that the theoretical interpretation of such forms of women's actions does not only imply the 'capability' and 'knowledgeability' of women in monitoring their own social actions through other actors but also includes other elements such as using their own perceptions (ref. to: Turner 1992 in Long 2001:18) and preserving their social identities as social actors in the agricultural labour force.

To weave the threads together, one of the central arguments this study came up with is that women migrants are not passive but gain power instead, since they benefit from the men migrants' strategic location in their (i.e. the women's) networks. This power can be explained in terms of the women making use of the men migrants' wide social horizons in order to penetrate the work sphere. Men migrants on the other hand acquire their centrality and power through the women who assign them to be their intermediaries, an argument which will be discussed more explicitly when discussing the 'gender relations' in this chapter. Moreover, women migrants' power and agency are embedded in their 'knowledgeability' and 'capability' in monitoring their own actions through enrolling other actors in their networks and in using their own insights. It is therefore, then, that these findings are considered as a contribution by this study to be added to the idea of Long's actor oriented approach.

5.3.3 Women's intermediation in transitive relations

It is evident in practice that men migrants do not provide the only connection, i.e. 'local bridge[16] or bridging function', between the women migrants and the men tenants. Rather it is evident, that a few women migrants found their way to less isolating relations with the tenants' community through manipulation of their social networks with women in the tenants' families. Similarly Dannecker (1999) pointed out that reconstruction of social realities of the women workers and its contextualization draw attention to small and local forms of resistance. These forms of resistance do not intend to overlook the existing gender order but to reshape the structures and create new room for manoeuvre (Dannecker 1999:2–3) through creating and developing new forms of social networks beyond the migrant's community level. Thus, women of the local community undertake direct work negotiations with women migrants instead of relying on the intermediation through men migrants. This clarifies that the intermediation process, which is imbedded in such negotiations, also exists in the women's social world since women of the local community represent the men tenants. Hence, women migrants through their own choice and interest to interact with women of the local community have found a space, be it deliberately or non-deliberately, in which to maintain their economic and social identity as agricultural workers. This way they also preserve the traditional and cultural discourses of their societies, in which they operate their labour, a reality that demonstrates their *"commitment to the cultural system"* (Nageeb 2004:44). It is due to this fact, then, that women migrants acquire some 'effective agency' through bridging the existing men intermediation and, as according to Granovetter (1973), manipulating their social networks with the help of women of the local community in order to achieve specific goals (ref. to Granovetter 1973:1370) in spite of the social disparity between the two groups of women. This social inequality can be attributed to the variations in ethnicity and class.

---

16 Bridge is a line in a network, which provides the only path between two groups to the extent that it is the only alternative for many people (Granovetter, 1973:1364–1365). Local bridge or bridging function is a quantitative term but is nonetheless used in a qualitative analysis.

The tenants' relying on women sharecroppers to carry out the process of cotton picking and the obligation of the women sharecroppers in shouldering this responsibility is a kind of reciprocal benefit that can also be interpreted as a gender specific cooperation. In this relation, on the one hand, the tenants, through their 'dependability' on women, secure their cotton output. On the other hand, the women's 'accountability' to their partners is one of the primary factors that guarantee continuity of the partnership, despite the fact that cotton is not included in the partnership. This should not imply that the women are simply under the tenants' influence but that the women who accept these conditions are also in need of the wage work. This is particularly evident in the fact that Bargo and Tama women do not oblige themselves to participate in the cotton picking process because it coincides with the groundnuts picking.

The women sharecroppers' offer of the priority of wage labour (i.e. cotton picking) to women of their own ethnicity thereby ensuring the feeling of intimacy and belonging, the 'cohesiveness' and 'overlapping' of their relations. Collection of cotton pickers can be explained in terms of 'interconnectedness' that smoothes the progress of creating new work opportunities and strengthening the relations for women in the seasons to come. This provides evidence for a process that Granovetter (1973, 1974) captured in his argument of the *"strength of weak ties."* He claims that people are more likely to find out about job opportunities through weak ties rather than from strong ties. The information concerned can be obtained through someone with whom you are acquainted but who travels in different circles (Granovetter 1974 and 1973). Thus, cotton pickers, who are not tied to the tenants (i.e. having weak ties with the tenants), will be tied to them in the coming season(s) through the possibility of finding work opportunities. This can also be explained as another form of 'transitivity', since women partners work as intermediaries between men tenants and women cotton pickers.

5.3.4 Adjacent actors: women migrants and the tenants

Conditions under which the women themselves negotiate their work with the men tenants without relying on intermediaries, as in the case of Beni Halba women, can be attributable to social network fragmentation among this ethnic group. Social network fragmentation is due to several cases of divorce and polygamy at the locality of the respondents from Beni Halba. Notwithstanding the existence of the social network fragmentation among this ethnic group, women have found ways to be actors. This social status fostered most of them to be independent and to acquire agency themselves. Moreover, their long stay in the Gezira area and their engagement in the process of cotton picking at earlier times, in addition to the other reasons mentioned above facilitate their direct contacts with the men tenants. These 'adjacent contacts' enable some of these women to acquire some agency that is manifested by their strong 'bargaining power'. A divorced woman from Beni Halba, aged 50, presents a special case of interest. She sets her and her daughters' acceptance of carrying out the cotton picking with one of the men tenants as a condition for getting a work opportunity on sharecropping in the coming season:

"When the tenant, our current partner, asked me to pick his cotton, I said to him, 'if you offer my daughters and I some feddan from your Hawasha to share with you, we will pick your cotton, otherwise we will not pick it'. We had picked his cotton for quite a long time before we became his partners and I know that he relies on us because our work is very good. That is why I said this to him. This is the way we became his partners."

This strong statement explains that some women as *"actors always face some alternative ways of formulating their objectives; organizing specific modes of action and giving reasons for their behaviour"* (Long 2001:18). Hence, this woman takes advantage of the tenants' 'dependability' on the women migrants in general for picking the cotton and, her 'knowledgeability that this tenant relies particularly on them (she and her daughters) due to the good quality of their work: *"I know that he relies on us because our work is very good"*. She takes these advantages in order to exert pressure on the tenant they deal with as a strategy through which they (she and her daughters) get another work opportunity, which they need in addition to the wage work. This is clear when this woman says: *"if you offer my daughters and I some feddan from your Hawasha to share with you, we will pick your cotton, otherwise we will not pick it"*. Giddens' (1984) argument, which puts the issue of 'dependability' as *"all forms of dependence offer some resources whereby those who are subordinate can influence the activities of their superiors [... and] in this way they are actively engaged in the construction of their lifeworlds* (7), *although the circumstances they encounter are not simply of their own choosing"*, (Giddens 1984:16 and Long 1992:24), suits this situation. However, since women who acquire such kind of agency are indeed social actors they should not be considered as subordinate or passive. Thus, women as actors, as has been noted by Long (1992, 2001), are actively engaged in the construction of their lifeworlds and are able to process the social world around them in which all the action takes place (Long 1992:24 and Long 2001:16). Furthermore, one should conclude here that this signifies that women exercise some kind of 'power' through using their

rights to demonstrate their 'negotiation power' when they need it in order to process their lifeworlds. Such form of action matches the meaning of the notion of 'effective agency'. Effective agency, which is identified when particular actions cause a change in pre-existing situations, requires organising capacities; it is not simply the result of possessing certain persuasive powers or forms of charisma (Long 1992:17 and 23). It requires then the strategic generation of a network of social relations and channelling of specific items (such as claims, orders) through certain 'nodal points' of interpretation and interaction. It is therefore essential to take into account the ways women employ as social actors or in which they are engaged in struggles over the attribution of social meanings to particular actions and ideas (ibid: 17 and Long 2001:17).
Despite the commonality of the existence of network fragmentation among Beni Halba, one woman at the age of 47 makes use of these 'adjacent contacts' by introducing other women belonging to the same ethnic group as new partners of her former partner (men tenant) with whom she terminated her partnership. This woman said:
"Yes, last year I introduced two women from Beni Halba to my old partner to work with him as sharecroppers in his 'Hawasha'. I also knew that they were looking for someone to work with. One of those women is my cousin and the other is her daughter."

Hence, changing the partnership is not just leaving a work place in favour of another, but also establishing a link with the previous place. Women use these ties as an advantage for others in providing them with work opportunities, i.e. the 'bridging function' in operation. Bridging function here means that these women migrants who changed their work place are the only path/connection between the new women partners/sharecroppers and the men tenants. Thus, the men tenants through their old partners (women) will be tied to other women (new partners) they were not tied to before. Hence, such form of 'interconnectedness' show on the one hand the significance of 'weak ties'. On the other hand, the 'interconnectedness' is considered to be a unique form of 'transitivity', since women as social actors use their 'knowledgeability' and 'capability' in monitoring their own actions, (Giddens 1984:1–16). This is manifest in manipulating their social networks in order to resolve problems of other women within the same 'cohesive subgroup', giving their reality of life some sense of constructive cohesiveness and social cohesion.
Furthermore, such ties are of importance not only in manipulation of women's networks in favour of others. Instead, they are on the one hand also channels

through which ideas, influence, or information about women migrants who are socially distant from the tenants and outside their social network circles (8), reach them (see Granovetter 1973:1370–1373). On the other hand, these links generate new networks for women with the men tenants and, according to Granovetter (1973), they form elaborate structures of bridging weak ties between the more coherent clusters that constitute operative networks in particular locations. From this point of view, then, weak ties are an important resource in providing for a higher level of mobility and they play an essential role in effecting social cohesion (Granovetter 1973:1373). Therefore, bridging weak ties and making use of indirect contacts, i.e. 'transitivity', are both highly relevant in women's social networks.

5.3.5 Negotiating gender relations (9): an image in transitive relations

To stress the importance of gender relations in the work sphere, it is important to point out that the Othering of women as a gendered social category essentially different from men formed a conceptual contrivance for the processing of women's social world, in which everyday life activities and gender interactions took place (Nageeb 2004:167 and Long 1992:23). Looking at women's search for work and their work negotiations from a gender perspective, one should note that gender relations in the migrants' communities are distinct, if their social life is categorised into private and work spheres. When examining the private sphere it is remarkable, that *"the physical and social 'gender segregation' of the sexes"* (Nageeb 2004:23) is moulding the outlook of the migrants. However, it is empirically evident, that the cultural discourse, under which women migrants construct their everyday life, does not set any barriers between the two gender categories within the migrants' communities at their work sphere. Under this cultural discourse, women discuss the work issues with the men migrants of the same ethnic group without the restrictions mentioned above and they are free to choose them as intermediaries. This signifies that ethnic identity is consciously and keenly felt by the women migrants in assigning their co-ethnic men to be their intermediary contacts with the men outside their ethnic groups (i.e. men tenants). It is important to note here, that the migrants' 'cohesive subgroups' are small groups within each of which, according to Granovetter (1973), each group member knows enough about every other member of the group to be able to decide whether to choose him and to meet him often enough so as for him to feel the need for such a decision (Granovetter 1973:1377). On these grounds it is useful to apply the 'transitivity logic' and certainly to enable women to acquire some agency in order to decide whom to choose among the men within the subgroup and whether to count on them as appropriate persons for being their intermediaries. This means that belonging to the same ethnic group to which women belong to, does not only qualify the men migrants to be intermediaries of the women migrants. It is the women who assign whom among the men of the same ethnic group they trust and on whom they have confidence in order to undertake the work negotiations in favour of them. Furthermore, the choice of network contacts is, according to Powel and Smith-Doerr (1994), guided by a matter of trust, of confidence in the information passed and the care with which the contacts chosen look out for women's interests in getting work opportunities (Powel and Smith-Doerr 1994:371). As a result of the choice of women to the men concerned to be their intermediaries, these men acquire prestige and power as compared to the other men in their respective 'ethnic group'. This interprets, as Nageeb (2004) argues, that the domain of women's social power is a meaningful in contrast to the domain of men's power (Nageeb 2004:24). Thus, women's power is complementary to that of men's. According to Boddy (1989) *"Each sex contextualizes the other; each taps a locus of power which the other cannot reach, each is symbolically dominant to its counterpart on a complementary plan. Each, in the process of engenderment, becomes empowered within a specific context"* (Boddy 1989:116). Furthermore, I argue that in addition to trust and confidence of women on the men whom they assign as their intermediaries, prestige and power as well, which are acquired by these men through women, foster the men concerned to undertake the work negotiations in favour of women. There are other central reasons beside this reason and the available cultural discourses that foster the men migrants to search for work for women and engage in undertaking the women's work negotiations. The socio-economic position of the migrants as poor people — who do not possess any means of production of their own, the most important of which would be the land — is one of the central factors that foster the men migrants to search for work for women and to act as intermediary contacts between the women and the men tenants. Hence, within the limits of scarcity of resources, men migrants perceive engagement of the women migrants in the agricultural work as a way of survival and maintaining the economic identity of the households. Nevertheless, I would like to maintain that empirical evidence shows clearly, that finding work opportunities for women is not restricted to increasing the household income as is reported by many scholars, but goes far beyond that into broader achievements, which will be discussed later in this chapter. Other reasons are associated with the properties of the migrants' 'cohesive subgroups', such as the feeling of intimacy, closeness, and a spirit of common destiny of the migrants' community. These factors keep the men migrants feeling responsible for searching for work and undertaking the work negotiations in favour of the women within their respective 'cohesive subgroup'.

Despite consideration of the men migrants' involvement in the search for work opportunities for women and in undertaking women's work negotiations as intermediaries, one cannot deny that these are new modes of control over women. These modes, regardless of whether they imply complete or partial control over the women concerned, reflect the existing gender order as well as the ideologies used to limit women's negotiation power. This also means that undertaking women's work negotiations is necessarily governed by gender. Thus, women's engagement in the work realm has, as Spring (2001) writes, not altered the gender ideologies altogether (Spring 2001). Nevertheless, I contend that, women are not passive — a fact that is evident in the way women construct the gender economic relations, which means that women can have relations with many men actors at the work sphere. Thus, women make use of the extensive relations of the men migrants with the men tenants not only as a way to maintain their economic identity as agricultural labour. Rather, this process also has socio-cultural dimensions in that women preserve the social and cultural discourses of their societies. Along the same lines, Bhachu (1993) contends that the women migrants do not consider their lifestyles as oppressed or subordinate, instead they accept the gender hierarchy because to them it is part of tradition. *"It is taboo and shameful for us, just like you."* ____ *"The man always goes ahead of the woman. Whenever there is any man from the tribe he speaks on behalf of the woman. These are our customs. It will never happen that a woman goes ahead of the man because this is a big mistake and a taboo"*. Rather, they have deliberately opted to interact with men through sticking to the traditional and cultural discourses of their societies (Meier & Knörr, 2000:10). Consequently, most women migrants opted to utilise the transitive relations. The primary reason behind the application of 'transitivity logic', which interprets the understanding of the cultural discourses, is the non-similarity between the groups of women migrants and men tenants shown in many different ways. The gender and ethnic identities are found to be key elements that explain such variations as well as *"the action of othering and gendering women"* (Nageeb 2004:167). This is in view of the fact that these factors of dissimilarity are linked to the traditional and cultural heritage which keeps them either entirely or partially 'isolated' from the men outside their ethnic groups. These facts explain the manifestation of 'gender segregation' between the majority of the women migrants and the men tenants.

Furthermore, it is to emphasize that these facts explicates that gender relations in view of 'transitivity' is associated with ethnic identity. The position of women in the work negotiations (i.e. partial or non participants) in which men migrants are actors is based on the ethnic identity of these women as well as their intermediary contacts. Thus, ethnicity is a key factor to understanding 'constructivism' of gender relations because it legitimates the position of both women and men migrants in the process of work negotiations. One should argue here that, despite the fact that the women concerned are presumably not involved in the process of meeting and getting along with strangers (Ketzer and Madison 1981:127), they acquire agency since they make use of the wide social horizons of the men migrants and of their extensive relations with the men tenants. Moreover, through manipulation of their social networks with women outside the migrants' communities in order to get work opportunities and by offering the advantage of their social networking with the tenants to women of the co-ethnic group as well as using their rights to demonstrate their 'negotiation power' when they need it in order to process their lifeworlds, women migrants, as Padmanabhan (2002) states, *"alter the existing gender relations by negotiations."*

As a result of what is explained, the structures of gender relations, focusing specifically on women migrants' search for work and undertaking work negotiations, are found to be different in the cultural realm and are also identified differently by the ethnic identity.

5.3.6 Analysis of findings

The analysis shows how women's social networks serve multiple purposes. Women's social networks facilitate a wide range of settings, be it wage work found through the men tenants or women acquaintances or sharecropping or land sub-leasing found either through male relatives or women of the local community. The key insights of women's social networks are that the available ways and contacts through which women acquire information about work and get work opportunities vary. These variations, therefore, explain the existence of the 'heterogeneity' in the way women migrants construct their social networks to achieve their goals as women labour. 'Heterogeneity', which is remarkable in the structure of diverse social relations including gender relations, shapes processes of information diffusion, search for work and work negotiations. 'Heterogeneity' is made plausible in the processes of information diffusion and in undertaking women's work negotiations where there appear to be considerable differences in these processes. These differences are evident within the same ethnic group as well as between different ethnic groups. These differences are attributable to the dissimilarity in the ways women construct their social networks within the existing diversity of the migrants' ethnic groups. In addition to that, women migrants' construction of their social networks is not confined to the frontiers of the migrants' social setting but expanded to reach other communities, e.g. the local community. Hence, when comparing the ways of undertaking the work negotiations and actions and social interactions of women migrants who belong to various ethnic groups, *"the diversity of African rural women becomes apparent"* (ref. to Padmanabhan 2002:178).

It has been found out that, the majority of women migrants' work is still conditioned by male and female spheres despite the fact that women's engagement in the agricultural work has become substantial. This is attributable to the traditional and cultural discourses in which women experience their everyday life in general and operate their labour in particular. Moreover, new modes of control over women emerged. These modes work under the discourse of taboo, which represents a form of tradition where the unmarried women have more limited space to negotiate work issues with the men tenants than the married women.

'Transitivity' or the 'weak ties' in the Gezira Scheme are between groups of people who differ from each other in various aspects i.e. existence of dissimilarity. They are from different regions of origin, belonging to different ethnic groups and consequently have different traditional and cultural discourses. In addition they belong to different gender categories and have different resources. Based on these differences the weak ties are applied in terms of 'transitivity'. The women migrants' strong ties to the men migrants and to the women of the local community bring them into interaction to get work opportunities. In such transitive relations the men migrants and the women of the local community act as intermediary contacts between the women migrants and the men tenants. The women migrants get their work opportunities and the strength of these week ties by means of a partner of a relative (in case of men migrants) and a relative of a friend (in case of women of the local community).

It is evident, that the application of 'transitivity logic' does not only permit the analysis of relationships within a single 'cohesive subgroup' but also of intergroups' relationships as well as of gender relations. It is therefore, then, that 'transitivity' has been shown to be a key property in women's social networks. This is evident particularly in the way women get access to information about work and find work opportunities. Thus, 'transitivity' specifies women's social networks as a common feature that explains women migrants' social structure. In addition to that it is considered as a leading force in the organisation of social groups. The reason that 'transitivity' is a compelling force can be attributed to the fact that the structures of the migrant groups living in the Gezira Scheme are so diverse. Lodging of the migrants in groups based on ethnicity explain that several ethnic groups and cultural discourses form those groups as clusters. The availability of cultural discourses of heterogeneous ethnic groups of the migrants living in the Gezira Scheme is also manifest where the work negotiations are governed by gender. On these grounds, ethnicity, gender and *"[...] Clusterability lead (naturally) to a consideration of the concept of transitivity"* (Wasserman and Faust 1994:243). In the view of these facts application of the 'transitivity logic' has therefore, become a necessity in the Gezira Scheme social context. Thus, an important finding is that 'transitivity' is not only associated with 'clusterability' as it is found in the social networks theory, but as well by considering the concepts of ethnicity and gender. Therefore, this finding is a new contribution by this study to the social network theory and analysis.

The theoretical importance of 'cohesive subgroups' lies in the social forces that operate through relative cohesion within the subgroup and through direct contacts among the subgroup members (women and men). These social forces aid women in using the 'transitivity logic' in order to be connected with the men tenants either where there are direct or no contacts between the two groups (ref. to ibid: 249 and 251). Using these ideas, the general properties of migrants' 'cohesive subgroups' that influence the formalisation of the women's social networks are ethnic identity, the social discourse associated with the ethnic identity, intimacy and belonging, closeness and 'reachability' (10) as well as operation of similar forms of labour. These commonalities, that explain how the women's relations within a single 'cohesive group' are associated, are decisive resources for ensuring work opportunities for women as one of the primary benefits of women's social networks.

Finally, although women migrants' engagement in the work sphere in the Gezira Scheme has not altered the gender ideologies altogether, women migrants could make use of the 'transitivity logic' either through their men relatives or through manipulation of their social networks with the women of the local community. Unlike the trauma associated with many cases where women are considered as subordinated, vulnerable, suppressed or excluded, this study comes out with a new understanding of women's social position and social networking. It provides evidence that women are not passive recipients but social actors in their societies instead. This is manifest where women benefit from finding work opportunities not restricted to increasing the household income, as has been reported by many scholars, but goes far beyond that into broader achievements. Such achievements can be cited as economic networks, mobility and a number of others associated with the acquirement of agency. These can be summarised as: women using men relatives' social networks with the men tenants, manipulation of women migrants' social networks with women outside the migrants' communities (i.e. the local community), accountability of women to their partners (tenants) to maintain the work relations, and, last but not least, women offering the advantage of their social networking with the tenants to women of the co-ethnic group. Hence, these achievements resulted in increased social power and decision-making. In addition to that, women influence the tenants' activities to get work opportunities, which can be interpreted as a strategy by which women exercise some kind of 'power' through using their rights to demonstrate their 'negotiation power' when they need it in order to process their lifeworlds. Moreover, as noted by Padmanabhan (2002), the five dimensions of agency women acquire, namely interactions and consequences, conditions, strategies and tactics (Padmanabhan 2002:155), distinguish their social networks. I therefore argue, that women acquire agency and are active actors, since it is evident that the women benefit from the construction of their social networks, a significant finding, which is considered as an addition to Long's actor-oriented approach.

To weave the threads together, construction of women migrants' social networks is not restricted to their own 'cohesive subgroups' and the migrants' communities. By means of formalisation and manipulation of their social networks women migrants have shown themselves to be able to intertwine their social networks with the other existing social groups in the Gezira Scheme.

5.4 Work relations in sharecropping

Sharecropping is the only form of partnership system between the tenants and the migrants applied within the Gezira Scheme. The migrants, who constitute almost all of the partners, own no means of production other than their physical labour. This sort of sharecropping is commonly applied in the cultivation of sorghum, groundnuts and vegetables. It is noteworthy that women migrants are sharecroppers only in the first two crops but not in the vegetables. The vegetables' sharecropping is a property of men. The tenant provides the partner with part of the tenancy where the partner is responsible for the entire work in the

field. Both share all the expenses to equal parts covering the costs of ploughing, seeds, fertilisers, cost of the combine harvester (in case of sorghum) and the sacs plus the taxes and *'Zakat'* (Islamic taxes). The taxes and *'Zakat'* are to be deducted immediately after the harvest from the total output. The net output of the crop afterwards should be split equally between the two partners.
There are fundamental and diverse reasons that lead to continuity or discontinuity of this partnership. Women respondents from different groups, on the grounds of their insight into this kind of partnership, agreed upon common factors that lead to its continuity.

The tenants, on the other hand, have their own perception. To continue the partnership, from the tenants' point of view, requires honesty and good performance of the partner as far as the actual work is concerned, which should result in high output and good quality. The tenants maintain that a sharecropper should stick to work with one tenant only; the migrants, however, are usually involved in multiple partnerships plus land sub-leasing. The tenants do not prefer such behaviour because to them it means distribution of efforts and low product. This is frequently a source of tensions and clashes between the tenants and their partners.
One of the men tenants, aged 50, expressed his opinion on the continuity of the partnership by saying:
"We prefer to work with a partner who works with only one tenant because we are keen to get a good yield. It happens sometimes that your partners assure you that they do not work with a tenant other than you but all of a sudden you discover that they work with another tenant too. This is actually a big problem to us. I myself passed through this experience and it was a bad one because when I found out that my sharecroppers, who used to be from Fellata, had another partner and just tried to discuss the issue with the man, it created a big clash between the two of us and, in the end I terminated my partnership with him."
A married woman from Bargo, aged 24, assures that the tenants' emphasis is only on the performance of the sharecroppers:
"Our current partner found out that our work was good so he asked us to stay and took another feddan. The 'Arabs' want the people who work well, clean and irrigate the 'Hawasha' perfectly and always look after the 'Hawasha'. He knows that I am an excellent worker since I was working with a woman tenant whose Hawasha is beside his."

It is also decisive to the tenants that the partners accept to work on the cotton fields. Under the Gezira Scheme regulations the tenant is solely responsible for the cotton. Some women sharecroppers are themselves obliged to carry out all the agricultural operations of cotton, all the way from sowing to picking the cotton. Such obligations strengthen the relations between the partners and encourage the tenants to accept to lend their partners money whenever there is a need and to be patient if there is a delay in the repayment. Some tenants oblige their women partners to pick their cotton. Women accept this obligation either because they are in need to the wage work or to guarantee continuity of their partnership. Nevertheless, women who cultivate groundnuts do not accept to pick their partners' cotton because it coincides with the groundnuts harvest. This refusal, which is found most commonly among the majority of Bargo and Tama women respondents, is no matter, as the tenants have a share as partners in the product of the groundnuts.

A few of the women respondents (5 %) complain that some of the tenants are either not keen to pay their wages earned by cotton picking or they delay these payments. Some of them, however, do not even complain to the tenants for fear they might discontinue the partnership. Nevertheless, this behaviour causes tensions between the partners and the tenants and sometimes it does in fact lead to the discontinuation of the partnership, particularly if the sharecroppers find other tenants to share their crop with or if they are already involved in another partnership that enables them to possibly increase the area of sharecropping. This possibility, as Powel and Smith-Doerr (1994) have noted, lies in the nature and depth of the relations (Powel and Smith-Doerr 1994:384) of the men migrants (sharecroppers or women's intermediaries) or women migrants with those tenants and the performance (of women and men) in the sharecropping. Hence, strong ties and good performance in carrying out the work bring about commitment that lasts for a longer period of time.

Most of the women respondents (75 %), on the other hand, perceive continuity of the partnership for several years as due to the good treatment of the tenants. This can be explained in terms of avoiding to put pressure on the partners by the tenants, by not supervising the work of the partners or giving orders, a kind of behaviour which the migrants hate very much. One can interpret this abhorrence as due to the utilisation of power by the tenants and their mistrusting their partners.
One of the men tenants by his following statement consolidates these women's insight regarding the issue of trust:

"It is not always easy to deal with your partners. These people are very sensitive and if you even come to the field just to see what is going on they immediately get the feeling that you do not trust them."

This is an example that reveals the way women justify why they continue to work with their partners for many years. A married woman from Misairia, aged 42, who works with her two daughters as sharecroppers stated:
"He is a good tenant to us. He does not create problems at work. He brings the seeds according to the agreement of our partnership. We either pay the plough's costs or he pays it. If he pays, he does not come to ask us about our share until after the harvest. He also does not come to us in the field to monitor our work. He only comes at the harvest time to pay the taxes and 'Zakat' because he is the landowner. He also waits for us until we go to him at the post-harvest time to do the calculations when we all bear the costs together and we deduct them from the return. He is kind to us. He cooperates with us. We are also honest in the work."

Based on my observations, the women migrants who are partners provide the households of their partners (the tenants) with part of their vegetable products, which they usually get for harvesting these crops. The women migrants justify this offer as these households belong to their partners.

5.4.1 Continuity or discontinuity of partnership

Judging the likelihood for success in the partnership requires different factors and circumstances that should be provided for by both parties. It is explained that most of the women migrants rely on the transitive relations to engage in the sharecropping with the tenants. However, I argue here, that simply mediating between women migrants and the tenants to be partners is not the end of the way of making a fortune for women. The partnership is susceptible to discontinuity, not only because the tenants' are 'central' since they control the land, i.e. 'centrality of land'. There are other fundamental and diverse reasons that lead to continuity or discontinuity of the partnership. Continuity of the partnership is a gesture of good relationship between the two partners.

Monitoring the sharecroppers' work by the tenants gives women sharecroppers and their male relatives the feeling that the tenants are 'prestigious' and do not trust them as well. Thus, tensions and clashes are inevitable outcomes of such behaviour. In most cases this signifies involvement of the men migrants (who either act as intermediaries for women or engage with their women relatives in the sharecropping) in the clashes with the tenants. On the other hand, whether or not the women, for their part, trust the tenants as partners depends heavily on the men migrants who act as intermediary personal contacts who, based on their own knowledge, assure women that those tenants are trustworthy (ref. to Granovetter 1973:1374). Quoting Grätz (2000): *"Stable social relations, ties of affection and common basic ethical assumptions are generally elements which generate trust, stabilise social networks and guarantee economic stability, especially outside formally-legal regulations"* (Grätz 2000:16). Therefore, 'trust', 'reliance', and 'confidence' of both parties in each other are decisive ethics and concepts in the work relations and considered to be an important feature of women's social networks. These concepts also became very significant in the analysis of other forms of women's work relations. Lachenmann (1998), for instance, asserts the usefulness of confidence and trust concepts in the 'modern' analysis of social organisation of the economy as the fundamental element of economic relations, which is a dimension of social embeddedness of female 'modern' economy as a new sociology of economics (Lachenmann 1998:7).

Continuity of sharecropping is deeply *"entwined in people's other social relationships"* (White 1992:63). The fact that women migrants provide the tenants' (partners') households with part of the vegetable products *"[...] indeed, represents the most perfect case of social capital being realized in material goods, and so a neat example of inter-household relations"* (White 1992:63) which foster continuity of the partnership. Provision of material resources is also evident in the acceptance of the tenants to give loans to the sharecroppers whenever there is need. The tenants' patience in cases of delay in the repayment and clearance of other financial issues (e.g. remuneration of the cotton pickers), which when overlooked can be the cause for exploitation of women sharecroppers who work as wage labour in the cotton fields, are all significant factors for the continuity of the partnership. This explains that the partnership is a two-way street since the relationships between the women migrants and the tenants have elements of a reciprocal benefit. Thus, changes in the partnership indicate shifts in the local forms of social relations that exist between the women migrants and the women in the tenants' families.

Good work performance that results in a high production volume is a fundamental factor for continuing the partnership from the tenants' side. It is preferable for the tenants to avoid having to engage in a multitude of partnerships and work relations. This is mainly to ensure concentration of efforts and good performance of the partner(s), which consequently lead to good production and a high productivity, and thus to a high degree of profitability. To stick to one tenant partner gives the partnership life, sustains it, and shapes the direction of the partnership. Consequently, these are the central reasons boosting the work relations between the tenants and the sharecroppers and they encourage both parties to continue in the partnership. On the other hand, if one or more of these factors are not available the partnership will be at risk. I here contend that social networks built on work relations arising for a specific purpose and when that purpose is not attained then these relations are 'transient' (11). What makes the movement from one partnership to another possible is the freedom of the women migrants to sell their labour owing to the process of 'free labour formation' in the Gezira Scheme (see note no. 6).

Notes

(1) The migrants call the people of the local community *"Arab"*. Hashim (2004) explains that the shades of the colour of blackness, which were generated in the Sudanese culture, were perceived as authentic racial differentiations. A Sudanese-bound criterion for racial colour was formed by which the light black was seen as an Arab, that is white or at least non-black. The jet-black Sudanese was seen as an African (Hashim 2004:19).

(2) Several reasons have been brought up by the people of the local community to justify the process of evacuation of the Bargo ethnic group from Baika village. These reasons can be summarised as the high number of , particularly Bargo, coming in during the 1980s, which led to a drastic increase in the number of those migrants who lodge in the village. This, consequently, caused pressure on the social services available in the village. Some villagers object to the settling of migrants among them. Those villagers justify this aversion by explaining how big the differences in the way of life, customs, traditions, and behaviour of the migrants and that of the people of the local community are. Some respondents among the Bargo ethnic group pointed out that the Arabs take a lot of consideration when dealing with them because they know that they are very powerful and that is why they have removed them from the village. For these reasons most of the people of the local community do not wish these migrants to be assimilated into their community. One could argue here that the policy of settling the migrants in camps surrounding the villages of the local community was set by the British rule in Sudan who established the Gezira Scheme and that all the post-independent governments of the Sudan followed the same principle. Since then and as a result of this policy the people of the local community have adapted themselves to this way of settlement. There were, however, a number of other reasons for the fact that the migrants could not be fully assimilated into the local communities. It is noteworthy that the Bargo group has complained to the Sudan Gezira Board (SGB) and the local government of that area. Thanks to the intervention of these two institutions, they have in fact established a camp in the near vicinity of the village concerned.

(3) 'Social distance' between two individuals in a network has been defined by Granovetter (1971) quantitatively as the number of lines in the shortest path from one to another. This corresponds to the definition of 'social distance' in graph theory (Granovetter 19971:1366). However, for the purpose of this study 'social distance' is defined as the non-existence of ties.

(4) According to the rules of the Gezira Scheme cotton is under the sole responsibility of the tenants. It is not allowed to include the cotton in other existing work relations and processes as sharecropping. This means that the tenant should carry out all the agricultural operations, starting from cultivation until handing over the product to the Sudan Gezira Board for ginning.

(5) Field Inspection Office: The Gezira Scheme is divided into Field Inspection Offices and each of these Offices is responsible for specific number of tenancies.

(6) As laid down in the Tenancy Agreement of the Gezira Scheme of 1927, the provision of labour is considered to be the responsibility of the tenants. *"When Karl Marx analysed capitalism, he called wage labour 'free' because workers own no means of production and are 'free' to sell their labour force as a commodity in the market without any form of coercion beyond the economic necessity of earning a living."* (Bernstein et al 1992:186)

(7) Lifeworlds: Long (1997) defined lifeworlds as an analytical concept when he developed 'An Actor Oriented Approach' at Wageningen Agricultural University. Lifeworlds are the realities that people adaptively construct for themselves. They are the sum total of the mental maps and models that people have built to allow them to cope in their environments and, as such, are made up of past experiences and personal shared understanding. The methodological importance of the lifeworld concept is that it explicitly acknowledges that people have different realities and renders understanding these realities a primary research activity. This is very different from more traditional approaches that put the main emphasis on the scientist's understanding of problems and solutions. (http://www.consecol.org/vol5/iss2/art13/).

(8) 'Social circles': Simmel (1955) called collectivities "social circles" (Simmel, 1955 in Wasserman and Faust 1994:292).

(9) Gender relations refer to dimensions of social relations, which create systematic differences in the positioning of women and men in social processes (Kabeer 1992:17).

(10) 'Reachability' refers to how easy it is for all people to contact one another through a limited number of steps: how easy is it, for example, for gossip, ideas or resources to be diffused through the network (Scott 1991:32).

(11) 'Transient' relations defined by Scott (1991) as the underlying relations and obligations, which persist for one or two activities. According to him the relations and obligations that arise for a particularly limited purpose are more likely to be transient, whereas he describes the relations that are constantly being activated in interaction as highly durable, kinship obligations for example (Scott 1991:32).

6. Women's strategies: collective work

6.1 An introduction

This chapter spells out the ways in which different groups of women as social actors manage to solve the problems arising within the work sphere by means of social networks. This entails analysing women's strategies, which are identified as diverse social practices and traditions that migrants, mainly women, carry out collectively at the work sphere.

Social practices of the migrants' communities are characterised by collectivities. Collective actions, and social solidarity are noticeable features among the social groups of migrants used in order to support each other at their work sphere. One should note that the social practices applied by the individual 'cohesive sub-groups' vary. Long (1992) argues that the interlocking of collective strategies of actors generates social forms and commitments that shape common possibilities for action (Long 1992:9). Women are considered as active participants and a compelling force in the collective work in the field. This collective work encompasses various shapes of social practices, two of which are locally called *'Musaada'* and *'Nafeer'*, in addition to collective harvest and interactions with in-laws.

6.2 *'Musaada'*

'Musaada' is an Arabic word meaning 'help'. It is a service that the migrants provide each other with in the field in a form of mutual help and a reciprocal solidarity. *'Musaada'* is mainly organised by women as a strategy for solving problems arising in the field whenever there is need for help. It is done in cases of problems like sickness, giving birth or any kind of work in the field that needs more labour. People that are close to the affected person(s) and belonging to the same ethnic group, most likely to some sort of 'clique', usually recognise the problem themselves due to their close ties and frequent contacts. Accordingly, they decide on their own and without any request from the affected person(s) to undertake the work in the field without any reward other than providing the same services if anyone within the 'clique' is in need of similar assistance. A married woman from Bargo, aged 24 years, who works as a sharecropper, explains the way they carry out *'Musaada'* as follows:

"[...] The same people I mentioned. It is mainly women who help but men sometimes help us. At home my mother cooks for me, when I am sick my people help

me, my sisters, my neighbours, my cousins, [...]. From each house they nominate one to help me in the field and I also help them if they are in need or have a problem [...]. We help our relatives for free, for example we help the woman from our tribe, if she has work, for free but for the 'Arab' we only work for money. We do not work for the 'Arabs' for free."

This sort of *'Musaada'* is common only among Bargo and Tama whilst Beni Halba apply another form of *'Musaada'*, which is organised either by close relatives of the person concerned on their own accord or by the affected person(s) who request physical help in the field from the people they are close with. In the latter case the affected person subsequently provides the group with a meal.

A divorced woman from Beni Halba, aged 47, who works as a sharecropper and a land sub-leaser describes the way they help each other in the field:
"Either we know the 'Hawasha', which needs 'Musaada', then we start working on it, or the person who needs 'Musaada' tells us about it. 5 to 10 women usually participate in 'Musaada'. Sometimes men join us in 'Musaada'. We assist each other when one has a lot of work in the field but when I feel sick I hire some people to assist me in the Hawasha. My daughter helps me with the work and I also hire men to open the water Jadawil (water canals) for me to get the water for irrigation. We, as Beni Halba, have only 'Musaada' without paying money but we prepare food for the people who do the work. We don't have 'Nafeer' but Bargo and Tama do. I don't participate with Bargo and Tama in their 'Nafeer'. My daughter has participated only once in the last year with Tama in their 'Nafeer.' "

However, another woman from the same ethnic group, at the age of 50, who stays in the same compound and works as a sharecropper represents a particular case. She states:
"I invite my neighbour in the 'Hawasha' from 'Kardafa' and her daughters to help us (her and her daughters) because we have good relation with each other and we share the same tenant. They also ask us to help them when they are in need for help. So, we help them and they also help us. [...] But we do not have such a relationship with Bargo, Tama, and Fellata."

In almost all cases the number of participants ranges between 3 and 10 persons, depending on the group size or the number of the close people. This signifies that *'Musaada'* is only common among the migrants from Chad. Some of the women respondents pointed out that this social tradition is more common among women where the majority of the participants are women and the rest are their sons.

6.3 *'Nafeer'*

'Nafeer' is a one-day collective group work, which is organised to help a member within a 'cohesive subgroup' in the field. It is organised by the member who is in need of *'Nafeer'* by inviting the other members of the subgroup. The invitation is usually done in terms of an announcement at least two or three days before the day of *'Nafeer'* in order to give he next person a chance to fix a date for her/his *'Nafeer'*. This is because *'Nafeer'* is a form of mutual collective work, as people do it for each other in a spirit of a reciprocal solidarity. It is traditional for the organiser of the *'Nafeer'* to prepare a meal for the participating group on the day of the *'Nafeer'* after the work is done.

The following examples show the women's points of view on how they support each other through the *'Nafeer'*. A married woman from Bargo, aged 24, who works as a sharecropper, explains the way they help each other in the field and the difference between *'Nafeer'* and *'Musaada'*.

"My relatives from Bargo and their children help me in the 'Khala' and I also help them. When the work becomes too much we carry out 'Nafeer'. We are all Bargo and the number of people who do the 'Nafeer' is about 12 to 15 persons but in 'Musaada' the number is only from 5 to 10. The ones who do 'Musaada' are close relatives but those who do 'Nafeer' are the people from our tribe."

A 28-year-old married woman from Tama who works as a sharecropper explains that *'Nafeer'* is a form of mutual and reciprocated work:

"We work for each other in the field by doing 'Nafeer'. We do 'Nafeer' for each other if someone has a lot of work to do and we especially do a lot of 'Nafeer' in the time for picking the groundnuts and cutting the sorghum (i.e. harvest time). One person from each household works in the 'Nafeer' because the rest should work in their 'Hawashat'."

When further asked whether it is guaranteed that the people do the *'Nafeer'* for each other she answered by saying:

"Yes, of course, if you work in the 'Nafeer' of the other people here in our village, they will inevitably work in your 'Nafeer'. Our condition here is the same, all the people here in this village belong to one clan, and we are all one family."

A 24-year-old married woman from Bargo, who also works as a sharecropper, explains the way they conduct the *'Nafeer'*:
"We help each other in the work and if we have a lot of work to do in the field we ask each other for help. You go and tell all the people in Dar Elsalam and I cook the food at home and bring it to them in the field. They do not come to eat at home. We help each other always for free, for God. This is the way we help each other."

Another married woman from Bargo, aged 30 and working as a sharecropper says:
"When there is 'Nafeer', the person (the organiser of *'Nafeer'*) *prepares food for the 'Nafeer' people. They don't take money, it is for free; we do it to help each other. When I am not participating in the 'Nafeer' I help in preparing the food for the 'Nafeer' people."*

A married woman from Misairia, aged 42, who works as a sharecropper said:
"We invite all people of 'Kardafa' (Misairia) in Daim Wad El Laithie and also a few with whom we have a good relationship from the other tribes in this village. Each invited household usually nominates a woman or a girl to participate. If I could not join the 'Nafeer' of someone for any reason, I either help the organiser of the 'Nafeer' in the preparation of food for the 'Nafeer' people or provide her with some foodstuffs."

The reasons for carrying out *'Nafeer'* are either abundance of weeds, which affects the production and productivity, the right time for harvesting groundnuts and sorghum which need to be harvested in time because otherwise big losses are inevitable, short-time or long-time sickness and scarcity of household's labour. The participants of *'Nafeer'* are women and men; however, women are the dominating force in the *'Nafeer'*, as it is empirically evident that the majority of the participants are always women. The number of participants ranges between 12 and 20 participants, depending on the number of the households engaged in the working force within the subgroup. Participation in such collective work is a household decision in that the household members have to appoint one of them, usually a young woman, to participate in the *'Nafeer'*, whilst the other members are to continue their own work in the field. As a rule the majority of the nominees (70 % to 80 %) are women and most of these are young.
'Nafeer' is common among Bargo, Tama and Misairia; at least, all the respondents from those groups assure that they carry out this social practice regularly. It is not a tradition with Beni Halba, Fellata and Hausa. Almost all of the women

respondents from Bargo and Tama stated that their *'Nafeer'* groups embrace only people from within the ethnic group, whereas respondents from Misairia mentioned that their *'Nafeer'* include a very few (2 to 3) women from other ethnic groups. A 40-year-old married woman from Misairia supports this understanding by saying:

"We invite people from our tribe and also from the other tribes here for our 'Nafeer' but even if you do not tell some people from your tribe and they just heard about your 'Nafeer', they immediately come and join your 'Nafeer' because these are your relatives, they are part of you. Your blood is not like the others."

Another empirical evidence shows that members of the same ethnic group usually carry out *'Nafeer'* whereas it is known to be very rare that different ethnic groups collectively participate in the *'Nafeer'*. This happens in the case of Misairia women due to their small number compared to the other groups in Daim Wad Ellaithie and because of the fact that their men have abandoned the agricultural work — a cause for them to seek help from the other ethnic groups to join their *'Nafeer'*. This is the way a Tama woman, aged 55, justifies this:

"We used to invite a few women from 'Kardafa' (Misairia) and from the other ethnic groups like Bargo but they do not join our 'Nafeer', that is why we avoided inviting them last year. 'Kardafa' in Wad Ellaithie also used to tell us about their 'Nafeer' and we offered them some of our daughters but we do not invite them to ours. We (Tama) are able enough to carryout our 'Nafeer' by ourselves."

It is important to note here that the majority (about 75 %) of Bargo and Tama women respondents assured that they do not participate in the process of cotton picking because it coincides with the harvest of the groundnuts, which these two groups undertake through organising *'Nafeer'*. The following statement of one of the Bargo women in a focus group discussion proves this:

"We do not work in the cotton picking because it coincides with the picking of the groundnuts. We pick the groundnuts by doing the 'Nafeer'. If we work in the cotton picking who will then pick our groundnuts?"

Beni Halba only organise *'Musaada'*, but the *'Nafeer'* is not recognisable among them. Thus, they only rely on 'Musaada' plus hiring wage labour. It is noteworthy that 80 % of Beni Halba women respondents are fragmented by polygamy and divorce and variations in personality. These reasons can also be cited to justify the acquirement of low spirit of solidarity among those women. As to all Fellata and Hausa women respondents, *'Musaada'* is not recognisable among them and they do not organise *'Nafeer'*. They rely on wage labour that they hire from other ethnic groups, e.g. Bargo and Tama in case of sickness or other problems causing a demand for more labour. A 44-year-old married woman from Fellata explains why she hires labour:

"I am Midangidah but I do not work in the 'Hawasha'. My husband and my daughters and my sons are the ones who work in the 'Hawasha'. I help them very rarely because I cook food and sell it to the school girls and boys. If the work in the 'Hawasha' is too much for my daughters and their father we hire labourers either from the Bargo or Tama. That is why I have to sell food to be able to pay the labourers' wages. [...] Our relatives here, the Fellata also hire labour if someone is sick or has no daughter or sons to do the work."

The reason that the women respondents from Hausa and Fellata give for not having *'Musaada'* and *'Nafeer'* is that it is only a minority of the women who are engaged in the agriculture labour force whilst the majority works in the tertiary sector. It is also remarkable that the mothers abandoned working in the field, leaving it to their daughters. They engage in the tertiary sector like animals' rearing and food selling in order to cover, besides others, the expenses of the wage labour in the field. This has put a lot of work pressure on women of the younger generation, whereas their brothers, who are in most cases educated, do not engage in the agricultural work in the field.

The results explained above demonstrate that *'Nafeer'* is not recognised by Beni Halba, Fellata, and Hausa. However, the study has found that some women respondents do in fact participate in the *'Nafeer'* of the Bargo and Tama and a few of them only recently started to organise *'Nafeer'* themselves. Those women respondents are young unmarried women from Fellata and Hausa. This is the way a young unmarried woman from Hausa, aged 19, justified the input of the young women from Hausa and Fellata in the others' *'Nafeer'* whereas they are not used to practice it;

"[...] My sisters, who work together with me in the field, and I have some friends (women) here from the girls of Tama and Bargo. When our friends invite us to their 'Nafeer', we join them. [...] We thought of organising 'Nafeer' our-

selves and the first time we carried out 'Nafeer' was the last season for picking our groundnuts."

6.4 Collective harvest

Collective cotton picking is one form of the collective harvest that some groups of women migrants, namely Bargo and Tama, apply. This social practice is carried out by a voluntary group of women belonging to a co-ethnic group or a single 'cohesive subgroup' who choose each other as a 'clique' to collect cotton. The purpose for this collective work is to collect the wages received for this collective wage work so as to enable the formation of 'Iddah' association or a savings box[17]. The savings box is used to support the very poor ones in their struggles whenever one (or some) of them is (are) in need of financial support. The primary objective of the 'Iddah' association is to have sets of utensils that are to be utilised by every member of the association in the social occasions. A 24-year-old married woman from Bargo who works as a sharecropper spells out the following:

"Here in Dar Elsalam, we work together sometimes in one 'Hawasha' like for harvesting a crop and then the sheikh collects the return and keeps it in the box from which he donates it if anyone (a woman/a man) is in need. This is also the way we form the 'Iddah' association."

It is empirically evident that the strategy that aims at formation of 'Iddah' association or formation of a savings box is widely accepted by the Bargo women, whereas Tama women respondents assure that they do this work only for the formation of 'Iddah' association. Other groups of women who belong to other ethnic groups have other strategies such as collecting equal shares of money to form their 'Iddah' associations.

The collective harvests of groundnuts and vegetables, mainly tomatoes and okras, which are not carried out through the *'Nafeer'*, are another form of collective work that exists among some groups of the migrants' communities. Vegetables and groundnuts are crops, which are included in the sharecropping and land sub-leasing. Vegetables sharecroppers and land sub-leasers are usually men migrants who rely exclusively on women migrants to carry out the processes of harvesting. Women are also a compelling force in the groundnuts picking. Whilst 60 % of the women respondents stated that they carry out the harvest of

[17] More details about the utensils' association and the savings box are found in chapter 7.

groundnuts through *'Nafeer'*, 30 % of the women respondents, mostly those from Beni Halba, carry out the harvest of groundnuts neither through *'Nafeer'* nor for wage. Instead they do the job collectively with each woman receiving one third of the total product she harvests. The same method is also applied in the harvest of vegetables, where 50 % of the women respondents from Bargo and Tama are involved in such collective work. Those women assure that they either use these products for their households' consumption or sell some of them on the markets nearby.

6.5 Social interactions with the in-laws

Women migrants' social interactions with their in-laws are shaped by the absence of their husbands from the localities of the migrants in the Gezira Scheme. These men migrants (the husbands) gave up on the agricultural work and migrated further from the Gezira Scheme area to work in the big cities. This phenomenon is more noticeable among the Bargo, since 75 % of the married women respondents from Bargo, who represent 80 % of the total number of women respondents from Bargo, are wives of migrating husbands. These women, as well as their husbands, originally belong to the same ethnic group, the Bargo, owing to the existence of intermarriages within this co-ethnic group. Although some of those migrating husbands are willing to come back in order to help their wives in the field, especially during the high seasons, the majority rarely comes back to help. According to the Bargo traditions, the wives of the migrating husbands remain under the authority of their in-laws who replace their sons especially in taking decisions concerning the work in the field. In addition to that, both women and their in-laws engage in co-operational fieldwork by providing each other with their labour resource. The following paragraphs are two narrations that demonstrate the way the Bargo women and their in-laws interact with each other socially when the husbands are away. A 19-year-old married woman from Bargo, who works as a sharecropper, explains how her in-laws are a source of support to her and at the same time become her guardians in the absence of her husband:

"My father-in-law — who is my uncle —, especially if my husband is not there, replaces him with regard to responsibilities towards me. For example, he helps me in transferring the water and he helps me in the work and if I felt sick he does the work in the field and he gives us money. If I need to move out of the village (camp) or to travel I also tell my father-in-law."

What is said by a married woman from Bargo, aged 24, who works as a land subleaser, about her social interactions with her in-laws shows how she co-operates with them in the absence of her husband. From this narration it is also clear how she lives under the authority of her in-laws who, for example, engage in the process of decision-making concerning the work and also control her mobility:

"My aunt (mother-in-law) lives here in Dar Elsalam. She is my neighbour. She has one daughter and two sons, my husband and his brother, but my husband does not stay here as most of our men work in Khartoum. I co-operate with my uncle (father-in-law) and my aunt and my mother. We help each other; for example my aunt and my brother-in-law and my sister-in-law help me in the field and I also help them. [...] I also see my uncle's (father-in-law) permission if I would like to go to somewhere here in the neighbourhood and if my uncle is not available I tell my aunt. [...] My uncle and his son do not let you go and sell something in the market. Yes, they do it for you, for example if I have sorghum or groundnuts to sell in the market of Wad Medani, they do not let you do it, instead they do it for you. [...] I also discuss any matter concerning work with my uncle and my mother-in-law. If my husband is available he is the one whom I consult but if he is not available, I consult my father-in-law and my mother-in-law and I listen to their advice."

6.6 Construction of collective strategies

Women's strategies and collectivity have different dimensions in which *"the multiple realities and diverse social practices of various actors"* (Long 1992:5) are identified. Women as social actors collectively construct strategies to manage their work and to solve the problems arising within the work sphere. *'Nafeer'*, *'Musaada'* and collective harvest are excellent examples for these strategies developed by the migrants. These social organisations consist of mixed gender where young married and unmarried women act as a compelling force and, *"with dwindling strength, older women drop out of the system"* (Padmanabhan 2002:149). Kertzer and Madison (1981), who studied women's age systems in Africa, have come to the same conclusion for the case of Southern Sudan. Collective activities are organised on the basis of age groupings even before age sets are formed. Women in the same age set living in the same compound are particularly involved in various collective activities, including the agricultural labour. However, women of the executive age grade (over 50) may call on the unmarried girls to perform communal labour (Kertzer and Madison 1981:123). Women carry out *'Nafeer'* for each other not for wages but for serving food as an alternative for payment. Hence, it is a strategy that is constructed in a form of mutual collective group work and in a spirit of reciprocal solidarity in order to solve the problem of scarce financial resources that hinder the migrants to pay wages for hired labour. The *'Nafeer'* process, in which the reciprocal relations are embedded, matches the argument of Scott (1991) about reciprocated relations that involve exchanges, and can thus be considered as 'directed' from one person to another (Scott 1991:31–32). The *'Nafeer'* is comparatively similar to the women's social organisations in other African countries, which indicates that this form of collectivity is a feature that is specific to women's social structure in rural Africa. Padmanabhan (2002), who studied the women farmers in Ghana, wrote, "*women might hire additional labour, but since the most expensive resource in agriculture is labour, paying wages is not a form of remuneration among group members. The resource-poor women are mostly poor for money. Women have recently begun meeting for group work and then abstain from reciprocal eating*" (Padmanabhan 2002:148–149). As an upshot of practicing *'Nafeer'* or *'Musaada'*, the problem of scarcity of money that is supposed to be paid, as labour wages is resolved; the work is done in time, which protects the product from the losses. The high production, which is one of the main objectives of the tenants, can be considered as a collateral for the helped person(s), for continuity of the partnership in the coming season(s). In addition to that, the significance of social networks among Bargo and also Tama in organising *'Nafeer'* for picking their groundnuts surpasses the wage work (i.e. cotton picking).

The initiation of *'Musaada'* as a collective activity is generally left to the initiative of women. Different women's 'cliques' initiate actions to help the affected persons within each 'clique' at different times (ref. to Kertzer and Madison 1981:116). Hence, provision of *'Musaada'* by the close women to the helped person (a woman) shows the existence of women's 'cliques'. This also demonstrates that *'Musaada'* is a property of women's 'cliques', whilst *'Nafeer'* is a property of 'cohesive subgroups'. Nomination of *'Nafeer'* participants within a 'cohesive subgroup' by the household members implies that the household sphere is not a private enclosure but has other dimensions associated with the work sphere. This signifies that the work and the household spheres are 'overlapping'. Furthermore, practicing of *'Musaada'* and *'Nafeer'* as forms of revolving and mutual collective work necessitates the existence of social obligations, loyalty and trust among the key actors. These properties are made available to the migrants' 'cohesive subgroups' since they are small groups in which each person knows all other members of the subgroup. In addition to that, the other properties of the 'cohesive subgroups' provide for linkages between the members of each single 'cohesive subgroup' very much like the bond of belonging to the same ethnic group, which is considered an important resource in the construction of collective actions. All these properties are considered to be a resource that ensures the availability of trust and social obligations among the actors necessary to undertake their social practices in a form of reciprocity and exchange relations. Such properties (trust and social obligations) prove that 'cohesive subgroups' and the women's cliques acquire 'social capital'. Quoting Padmanabhan (2002): *"The establishment of a working group requires social capital to maintain group coherence and the prospect of at least returning labour in kind"* (Padmanabhan 2002:149).

Since *'Nafeer'* is a property of a 'cohesive subgroup', the existence of a dense network of ties within a single 'cohesive subgroup' derived from the properties that bind its members *"mitigate in circumstances where trust and norms of reciprocity are found in plentiful supply"* (Powel and Smith-Doerr 1994:393). Trust and other forms of social capital, such as social obligations, are particularly interesting, because they are moral resources that operate in a fundamentally different manner than physical capital. The supply of trust increases rather than decreases with use (Powel and Smith-Doerr 1994:385). It is therefore, then, that the women migrants' share of the rural destiny and 'durability' (1) of their social networks of relations proves the presence of operable trust. The concept of trust is, consequently, found to be very significant, since the participants of *'Nafeer'* rely on each other in carrying out this collective reciprocal work. Thus, mutual trust is found to be central in practicing *'Nafeer'* among the members of a single 'cohesive subgroup'. It is also evident that *"ethnicity and trust-building are closely linked"* (Macharia 1988:22), since the members of a 'cohesive subgroup' belong to the same ethnic group and since carrying out *'Nafeer'* is a property of an ethnically homogeneous group. Hence, this study contends that the strength of social networks among people of the same ethnic group in practicing their social traditions such as *'Nafeer'* and *'Musaada'* is evident. This is attributable to the properties that associate the members of the 'cohesive subgroup', the bond of belonging and the concept of mutual trust among those members.

Women's collective harvest for getting one third of the harvested groundnuts in case of Beni Halba (women and men) is a women's problem solving strategy since the *'Nafeer'* is not recognised among Beni Halba. Collective harvest of vegetables, e.g. tomatoes, by the Bargo and Tama women in exchange for one third of the harvest is another strategy women apply. Since vegetable production is a men's task, which implies that it is a 'gender specific' work, and since the *'Nafeer'* is a reciprocal collective work, women do not carry out the vegetables harvest for free. Men migrants on the other hand cannot afford to pay their social obligations in cash, for example to employ women laborers, instead, they rely on exchange women labor with part of the harvested product. They might, therefore, profit more from these relations (Refer to Lachenmann 1997: 50). Consequently, negotiations between the genders within a co-ethnic group become inevitable in which *"women show personal commitment, since the voluntary association has no other foundation to stand on"* (Padmanabhan 2002:149). This commitment emanates from the existence of a dense network of ties that bind the members of a single 'cohesive subgroup' and from the ability of women to utilise these ties effectively (ref. to Wasserman and Faust 1994:393). These women's reality promotes the diffusion of common understanding and principles, thereby facilitating the agreement of women to get their wages from the men migrants in terms of one third of the harvested amount of groundnuts and vegetables. One can contend here that the commitment of both actors (women and men migrants) to this strategy is considered as a form of a gendered specific cooperation within the 'cohesive subgroup' to which they belong. Developing a strategy such as this through this mode of women's collectivity is a way out for these women on the one hand, to get more work opportunities. Women could make use of their share in the harvested products to supplement their households' subsistence needs and their households' income as well. The men migrants on the other hand, could get out of the trap of scarcity of remuneration resource. By the application of such strategy the men migrants manage to secure the scarcity of financial resources that abandon them from not being able to pay the wages in cash for the harvest labourers who are exclusively women.

Furthermore, women use their human resources and social identity as agricultural wage labour to invest their collective wages in establishing their savings boxes and 'Iddah' associations. Thus, women migrants proves that they are social actors in solving their problems and lessening their struggles in their private sphere under the principle of co-operating within the work sphere. Such a strategy proves that women are knowledgeable and capable actors and that they use their social networking in order to acquire agency and manage their problems within the economic coercion, which they experience in their everyday life. These fit with Giddens' (1984) postulation regarding the concept of agency, which embraces two principal elements, the 'knowledgeability' and the 'capability' of the social actors. Hence, women as social actors construct their own strategies by which they use their human resources, in order to get the work done collectively and, at the same time, to manage their struggles and solve their economic problems. Hence, women have the capacity to process social experience and to devise ways of coping with life, even under the most extreme forms of coercion (ref. to Giddens 1984:1–16). In another line of argument, women found their way through their focussing on their social networks, which they use to construct their collective actions by which they solve their social and economic problems. This interprets that their economic activities are considered as complementary to their social networks. This line of argument goes along the same lines of White (1992) who studied "Gender and Class in Bangladesh": What is however most striking, is the way that women have taken the constraints and turned them to their own use. These constraints foster women's concentration on their social networks and relationships for 'social capital' and these come to represent the crucial locus of female power, in a society of which networking is the central underlying principle (White 1992:93). Women's ability to solve their problems by using their social networks signifies that women gain their power from their social networks and collective actions. Thus, women show loyalty, commitment and coherence to their ethnic group, signifying a strong coherence within the ethnically homogeneous group.

It is realised that homogeneity in the ethnic background is a very decisive resource in the construction of collective strategies and in carrying out collective work. One could argue that 'clusterability' of the migrants in scattered settlements occupied by co-ethnic groups allows for coherence within these groups and for the construction of collective strategies like the *'Nafeer'* and collective harvest in an ethnically homogeneous society. It is also crucial to note here that the existing ethnic groups differ in their responses and in their actions and social interactions, although they live in structurally similar circumstances and relatively homogeneous conditions (Long 2001:11). Beni Halba, Fellata and Hausa women show less solidarity in comparison with the Bargo, Tama and Misairia women, with whom mutual help and spirit of reciprocal solidarity are deeply embedded in the social actions and interactions. This is attributable to the fact that these three ethnic groups have a rich organisational life while the others are socially more fragmented, which means that their social life is characterised by 'social networks fragmentation'. In addition to that, some social practices like *'Musaada'* take different shapes rooted in the ethnic group.

Women migrants' social structure and social organisation emerge from their social interactions that take place between several kinds of actors. Long (2001) supports this view noting that actors include not only those who are present in given adjacent contacts but also those who are absent but who nevertheless influence the situation, affecting actions and outcomes (ibid:13). Good examples of those actors are the migrating husbands who either depend entirely on their wives to maintain their economic identity at their second home in the Gezira Scheme or who are prevented from coming back frequently by their work circumstances and the social networks at their work place. Similarly, Santen and Schaafsma (2000) state that *"it is very important to point out that a migrant man can never be certain as to the exact length of his absence. This is contingent on finding employment immediately, which in turn depends in his social network in town"* (Santen and Schaafsma 2000:42). Thus, their being integrated in another social world leads to weakening the men migrants' social interaction with their original community.

What concern us here more is that the women of migrating husbands become more active and shoulder the responsibility of the work when their husbands are away. It is noteworthy that solidarity of women migrants within each 'cohesive subgroup' builds on numerous ties connecting these women and causing them to form 'cliques'. Some of those ties are the traditional social ties such as in-law relationships. In this manner, the loss of the husbands' labour within the migrants' communities, as described by Santen and Schaafsma (2000), is compensated by women and their in-laws who relieve them of the burden of having to manage the work in the field all by themselves (ibid. 45). Thus, however, the in-laws have control over these women in many respects. It is found out that migration of the husbands provides women with different strategic dimensions, although they have not become entirely independent in their decision making process and in the construction of their social networks. Nevertheless, women actors make use of the authority of their in-laws to cooperate with them in a reciprocal manner, a fact that lessens the women's workload. In addition to that, women benefit from the existing social networks, especially in case of problems, e.g. sickness and the need of labour resource, by being among their in-laws and the ethnically homogeneous community originating in the same region.
To conclude, through their particular social networks with their in-laws, women migrants (the Bargo) involve in a reciprocal solidarity through providing each other with their labour resource. Hence, women migrants' particular social net-

works with their in-laws form 'instrumental' and purposeful types of social interactions that embody joint transfer of 'material' and 'non-material' resources.

6.7 Gaining knowledge from others' experiences: a process of social change

Despite the fact that *'Nafeer'* is usually a form of a reciprocal solidarity, which is most likely practiced within an ethnically homogeneous group, there are some discrepancies between the norm and the practice associated with a process of social change. This is made clear in the emergence of new networks of relations in terms of the competence of some women (and also men) of the younger generation of Fellata and Hausa, as new actors in others social traditions, who have shown themselves able to generate friendship relations with folks of the same age from the other ethnic groups, namely Bargo and Tama. This helped the women of the younger generation from Fellata and Hausa to take advantage of the available social and cultural discourses of Bargo and Tama in organising their own *'Nafeer'*. Hence, this coincides with Long's (2001) argument when he says: "*The strategies and cultural constructions employed by individuals are drawn from a stock of available discourses that are to some degree shared with other individuals, contemporaries and perhaps predecessors*" (Long 2001:18). Hence, one should emphasise here that friendship, as a form of social relation, is an entry to other cultures as it is a means of exerting influence, gaining knowledge and transferring experiences of others by sharing their social and cultural discourses, and the subsequent application of their social traditions.

It becomes possible then for individuals and entire groups, between whom there have been no clear links and no grounds for establishing relative social ties in the past, to build social relations and to engage in joint activities in their mutual interest (Kertzer and Madison 1981:127). Furthermore, the joint participation, i.e. the 'social circles' of the younger generation of Fellata and Hausa with their contemporaries from Bargo and Tama, does not only provide them with the possibility to develop ties or to help the others. It also offers them the opportunity to learn how the others use their social networks as a strategy to construct their social traditions in terms of collective work. To conclude this part of the discussion, the construction of social networks between various ethnic groups and carrying out joint participation among them is an absolute necessity for gaining knowledge from others' experiences and a means for resolving women's problems. Such findings support the assumptions of the actor-oriented approach regarding the capability of actors even within severely restricted social spaces, formulating decisions, learning from others' experiences and acting upon them

(Long 1992:24–25). To conclude this part of the discussion, construction of social networks by women from heterogeneous ethnic groups and carrying out joint participation is an absolute necessity of gaining knowledge from others' experiences and a means of resolving women's problems.

6.8 Construction of 'social heterogeneity'

From what has been explained, it becomes evident that different strategies that are constructed by different ethnic groups and dissimilarity in the ways of social organisation between 'cohesive subgroups' and even within a single 'cohesive subgroup' prove the existence of the 'social heterogeneity' that distinguishes the women migrants' social reality. It is therefore, then, that 'heterogeneity' of women migrants' social forms is a common feature of their social reality despite the commonalities of the properties that distinguish the migrants' 'cohesive subgroups' and the similarity of the circumstances in which they live and perform their labour in the Gezira Scheme. This provides evidence for the explanation of the actor oriented approach that enables different responses in similar structural circumstances, even if the conditions appear to be relatively homogeneous, a feature that reflects the meaning of 'social heterogeneity' (Long 2001:11 and 21). 'Heterogeneity' of social forms, within and between 'cohesive subgroups' in structurally identical conditions, shows the effectiveness of the structure of women's social networks. It also demonstrates 'knowledgeability' and 'capability' of different groups of women migrants and also satisfaction of women within their 'cohesive subgroups' in organising specific modes of action to cope with their struggles and problems to facilitate the achievement of their goals and maintenance of their social identity as women labour. Likewise, Long (2001) contends that, women's social reality is built upon various types of discourses, however, their choices are restricted, they are social actors in constructing their own strategies and they always find alternative ways of formulating their objectives and of organising specific forms of actions (ref. to ibid:18). Formulation and construction of strategies become feasible for women through using their social networks. This proves that the interlocking of women's strategies and collective work within their 'cohesive subgroups', as Long (1992) argued, generates social forms and commitments that shape common possibilities for action (Long 1992:9).

6.9 Sources and effectiveness of reciprocal social solidarity

Social life is never so unitary as to be built upon one single type of discourse, it follows that, however restricted their choices, the actors always have some alternative ways of formulating their objectives, arranging specific modes of action and giving reasons for their behaviour at their disposal (Long 2001:18). Consequently, the women respondents, particularly the ones from Bargo and Tama, perceive the sources of reciprocal solidarity, that are built by mutual work and activities, as traditions of social relations they have inherited and that have their roots in their original community based collective experiences. Nageeb's (2004) following writing suits this situation: As the women indicated, women's spatial practices were based in tradition, what was defined by women as "history" and "roots". For women, the relation between this history and these roots was the cultural and traditional heritage signifying women's social and cultural identity (Nageeb 2004). However, I argue that construction of women's lives through reaching decisions to carry out mutual work or any reciprocal activity is associated with a stock of reasons other than inherited features. Likewise, Hindess noted that capability of collectiveness entails use of types of available cultural discourses and differentiated knowledge and resources available to actors of different types and not simply inherited features of the actors (Hindess 1986:117–119 in Long 2001:18). This argument is made plausible by empirical evidence. Furthermore, I argue here that those reasons, which are the sources of solidarity, can be considered as properties that characterise the migrants' 'cohesive subgroups' and have influenced women's social networks formalisations. These properties are ethnocentricity (i.e. assimilation into the same ethnic group) and belonging to one region of origin, 'reachability' and 'closeness' (due to lodging of the migrants in one place), intimacy, operating similar forms of labour and acquisition of no resources other than their human resource. Such properties, as Padmanabhan (2002) pointed out, create a specific pool from which each one can ask for helpers (Padmanabhan 2002:148) and generate mutuality of ties. Hence, these properties, by acting as principles of social solidarity and social grouping in a society (Kertzer and Madison 1981:128), stimulate, reinforce and maintain the feeling of solidarity among women. One should note here that these properties draw attention to the existence of 'homogeneity' in various ways. This evidence of 'homogeneity' is similar to that of Granovetter's when he analysed *"the strength of weak ties."* The stronger the ties connecting individuals, the more similar they are in different ways (Granovetter 1973:1362). Thus, solidarity is built on these ties and connected with, as outlined by Kwiecinska (2001), a spirit of common destiny of rural community (Kwiecinska 2001:120). Developing the mutual work and activities in women's everyday contacts within their 'cliques' and 'cohesive subgroups' manifests such solidarity.

Sharing existential space, group identity and a spirit of a common destiny generates mutual help and reciprocal solidarity, among women migrants in particular and among the 'cohesive subgroups' in general.

6.10 Ethnic differences

Differences in the features of the women's social organizations and in the degree of their mutual help and solidarity exist between women migrants from different ethnic groups. This has been found as a social reality despite the existence of generalized reciprocity and social solidarity that mould the outlook of the women migrants from different ethnic groups. Bargo and Tama women are distinct in many ways compared to the other ethnic groups of migrants in the Gezira area. They have a rich organizational life in terms of organizing easily and collectively to achieve their goals and interest as agricultural labor. This specificity of Bargo and Tama, which is embodied in their collectivity and solidarity, can be explained by a number of reasons. Firstly, some of these reasons are linked to the historical background and events that they passed through. Their migration is associated to ecological, economical and political reasons that led to their impoverishment. This disadvantageous position fosters them to bind and construct social solidarity. A woman from Tama said: "W*e have learnt this since the years of war in Tchad, we all help each other"*. Secondly, women of Bargo and Tama in particular acquire 'power of agency' more than women of the other ethnic groups. By means of their 'effective networks', these women generate resources that are considered as a 'social capital', even among those lacking physical capital within their 'cohesive subgroup'. Hence, such an effective form of collectivity that exists among these specific groups of women as Coleman (1988) writes; constitutes especially important and a powerful form of 'social capital' since the members of the collective groups should forgo self-interest and act in the interests of the collectivity. A norm of this sort, reinforced by social support, and other rewards, is the 'social capital' (Coleman 1988: S104) that builds and strengthens the 'cohesive groups'; maintain their social struggles and social identity. These purposive organizations that consist of women as 'cooperate actors' who share some elements in common within specific social structure, are tied to each other by relations that constitute 'social capital'. This existing 'social capital' is considered as valuable resource for women in facilitating certain collective actions (ref. to ibid: S98).

Further, A vivid illustration of how women generate resources was made in the analysis of collective work (ref. to Powell and Smith-Doerr 1994: 374), even in the absence of men. Bargo and Tama women form alliances through their traditional relations, e.g. in-laws, to obtain higher level of support, a form of social organization that is rarely exists among other groups of women migrants. In the absence of their husbands, the fathers or brothers in-law carryout the tasks of selling the women's products in the market which is evident, citing Padmanabhan (2002), to be strictly gender-sequential like opening the water canals for irrigation by men (ref. to Padmanabhan 2002: 150). Thirdly, according to Granovetter (1973) variations in culture are often cited to explain such differences (Granovetter 1973: 1373) in the features of women social organizations and the degree of their mutual help and solidarity. Fourthly, almost all the Bargo men, who migrate to work in the cities come back regularly to help their wives or other women in their families in the field. Tama men are engaged in the agricultural work (This information is at least accurate in the empirical research settings). Thus, the existing 'gender specific' cooperation among these groups shows that women and men interact socially in order to reach common goals. The potential outcomes of the collectivity and solidarity of Bargo and Tama can be attributed to their intimacy and their close and intense ties, which are manifested by their coherence and 'overlapping' of relations. This is similar to what has been noted by Powell and Smith-Doerr (1994), i.e. the existence of a dense network of ties and the ability to utilize these ties effectively (Powell and Smith-Doerr 1994: 393) an evidence that made plausible in their financial satisfaction between the agricultural seasons and resolving all kinds of problems within their 'cohesive subgroups'.

Some of the ethnic groups under study (Fellata, Hausa, Beni Halba and Misairia) have poor organizational life in contrast with Bargo and Tama. The reasons for this difference are attributable to the social and historical events, which led to the spectrum of social change. Fellata and Hausa who migrated to the Gezira area in the first half of the 20th century are considered as the first groups of migrants who settled in the GS. Their being the first migrants in the scheme area generates a big social change, which consequently alters the pillars of their social structure over time. Their settlement in the Gezira area for long time offer some of them the opportunity of buying tenancies (20) which signifies a shift from wage work to tenants. However, most of the women of the second and third generation of these two ethnic groups abandoned the agricultural work and involved in the non-farming activities. This resulted in the involvement of a few of these women in the agricultural work. These are mainly the women tenants or their daughters. Their access to the tenancies and involvement in the non-agricultural activities generates sources of a proper income to these women and their families. In another line of argument, one could contends that the occurrence of this social change among these two ethnic groups generate poor organizational life in terms of less mutual help and solidarity as compared to Bargo and Tama.

According to Beni Halba, early migration of women of this ethnic group to the Gezira area causes several cases of divorce and polygamy. This social status generates social networks fragmentation among the migrants of this ethnic group. Misairia as a Sudanese ethnic group used to come during the off-season of their subsistence traditional agriculture in the west of Sudan, to the Gezira Scheme as seasonal labour on cotton picking. Misairia men as Sudanese ethnic group have found better work opportunities in the urban sector as compared to Bargo men. Thus, they provide the women with financial support from which they would cover the agricultural costs.

Notes

(1) 'Durability': Referring to Scott (1991) 'Durability' means how enduring the underlining relations and obligations activated, in particular the connections, are. Those, which are constantly being activated in interaction, are durable, whilst those, which persist for one or two activities, are transient (Scott 1991:32). Migrants' social networks that build on ethnic relations are durable obligations that last for the entire life of the person concerned while work relations that arise for a particular limited purpose are transient. This is the case with sharecropping, since the partner is free to sell her/his labour to other tenants relying on a process of free labour formation.

7. Women's private sphere: a construction of 'social security'

7.1 An introduction

Women migrants in the Gezira Scheme confront different forms of social struggles in their everyday life. These women are actively engaged in the construction of their own social worlds, although the circumstances they encounter are not simply of their own choosing (Long 1992: 24). By means of their social networks, these women engage in several collective actions and social activities in their private sphere, which are manifest in the construction of their own *"social and economic strategies of security"* (Lachenmann 1997:50) and mutual social support. This chapter examines the social networks of women migrants in their private sphere by analysing the types of social support women render to each other. The analysis also underlines how these women cope in solving the problems arising within their private sphere by means of their social networks. On these grounds, the structure of this analysis touches crucially upon the issue of 'traditional social security' and necessitates its consideration as a key concept in the analysis. According to Lachenmann (1997) 'traditional social security' mechanisms are always based on diversification of production and division of labour, as well as on complex social relations, of which gender relations and women's networks form a very important part. This study focuses on the 'traditional social security' which is based on women's social networks. 'Traditional social security' is one of the visible features of the women migrants in the Gezira Scheme, which are found to be of multiple shapes and purpose. Since women have their own security mechanisms (ibid.) women migrants' 'traditional social security' is examined in terms of women's informal associations as strategies for security and mutual social support in social occasions. The analysis also emphasizes women's 'social security' in the context of inter-household relations. This is defined in terms of social support for the needy, which is evident in the lending of money to them and the carrying out of their domestic tasks. Sharing of food and other material items and free lodging of new migrants and guests are also explained in the context of inter-household relations.

Since women construct their security in a social world of their own this chapter spells out the issue of gender 'constructivism' as well as a gender specific 'social security'. It also highlights the social ties existing between women in terms of traditional relations and formation of women's 'cliques' as a significant foundation of the 'traditional social security'.

7.2 Women's social world: negotiating gender construction

Examining women migrants' everyday life and the construction of their social networks draws attention to the existence of cultural boundaries between the social set-ups of the two gender categories. Migrants of both sexes live in similar circumstances but gender creates a division of the migrants' social world. This gender 'constructivism' is associated with the available cultural discourse of the existing migrants' ethnic groups. In other words, ethnic construction brings about 'constructivism' of the cultural discourse of these groups and subsequently that of their gender. This is evident in a clear dichotomy between the social worlds of the two gender categories. The 'gender segregation' in the migrants' social life influences women as actors in the construction of their own social worlds (ref. to Long 1992: 24). Consequently, this construction demonstrates that women migrants' activities are not limited to their work sphere but extend to other activities that are related to the discipline and regulations of their social life. Thus, women's private sphere remains significant for women's lifeworlds. It enables them to construct their social networks in a 'gender specific' social world via which they achieve their own social goals. Nageeb's (2005) writing about women's private space addresses this situation. It is significant for the women's sense of being able to control their own social lives. To put it differently, women's private space enables women to practice their social power in controlling their space by eliminating the presence of others whose presence would shift the definition of private space to a public one (Nageeb 2005: 186).

Evidence shows that women migrants belonging to a single 'cohesive subgroup' live in a bound social set-up parallel to that of men. In some cases, these social set-ups encourage women to construct their social networks across the 'cohesive subgroups' to which they belong. This is demonstrated by the existence of enormous 'gender differentiation' and 'gender segregation' in the migrants' social realities. These modes originate from the traditional and cultural discourses that mould the outlook of the migrant communities, and are designed to construct women's social reality and limit women's options. What is striking here is that these constraints drive women to build a 'gender specific' social world of their own. Thus, in their own social world women are able to demonstrate their power in constructing webs of networks of social relations to reach common goals.

7.3 Informal social associations

Women's informal social associations can be defined as non-institutionalised associations that women form on their own without their being related to any official authority. Women establish these associations from their own funding without a link to formal financial institutions like banks.

'Sandoug'* and *'Iddah' are the two major women's informal associations identified in this research. *'Sandoug'* is an Arabic word meaning a box. It is known among the Sudanese women as well as the women migrants as a rotating savings box, established by women with an economic objective (2). However, the sort of *'Sandoug'* that this study focuses on is a new form established by the women migrants. This *'Sandoug'* serves a different objective for the migrant women than the traditional objectives of the rotating savings box. Women migrants establish *'Sandoug'* to provide financial support to the poor or whoever is in need in the women's 'cliques', or women in the same 'cohesive subgroup'. It is important to realize that women migrants define a poor woman as one who does not have money to prepare *'Karamah'* or to buy medicine. For the *'Sandoug'* to function women collect an equal amount of money on a monthly basis from the members belonging to one or more than one 'clique' in a single 'cohesive subgroup'. Traditionally, a member is nominated as keeper of the *'Sandoug'*. However, the Bargo women keep their *'Sandoug'* with the *'Sheikh'* of the camp. Whoever is in need of financial support explains her case to the Sheikh. In order to keep the box running, Bargo women collectively carry out wage labour for a few days and keep the total return in the *'Sandoug'*.

A married woman from Bargo, aged 24, explains the way they established their *'Sandoug'* and keep it functioning and how the needy get support:
"We collect money and keep it with the 'Sheikh' and give it to anyone of us who needs help. The 'Sheikh' has another box. Here in Dar Elsalam we sometimes work together in one 'Hawasha' like harvesting a crop and then we collect the money, which we get from this work (returns) *and give it to the 'Sheikh' who keeps it in the box. He gives out the money if a woman is in need. If it happens that someone has an occasion she goes to the sheikh and explains the problem or the need and, the 'Sheikh' gives her money from the box."*

A unique case is a woman from Zagawa, aged 29. She laments that the women migrants do not have access to 'formal social security':

"[...] We are not given 'Zakat', which should be given to the widows and needy people. We are not given it because the 'Arab' are responsible for distributing the - 'Zakat' money, although we need and deserve it because we have been living here for quite a long time."

In Daim Wad El Laithie, Hausa and Fellata women who either engage in agricultural work or in the non-farming activities have a savings box with an economic objective. However, the financial support through the saving boxes of the other ethnic groups in the compound has influenced Fellata and Hausa women to set a strategy for the establishment of a similar collective savings box. The objective of this box is to act as source of social support in cases of sickness, travel or any situation needing financial support.

A married woman from Fellata at age of 44 explains how the other women influence them to devise a plan for establishing a collective savings box. She explains the objective for establishing the savings box:

"We would like to establish a 'Sandoug' like the women of the other tribes like Bargo and Tama who have solidarity with each other. We discussed this issue one day in the field and have already agreed to make our own 'Sandoug'. We would like to use this 'Sandoug' for the needy ones from Fellata and Hausa, it would help the sick and provide tickets for those wishing to travel."

Unlike the case of Fellata and Hausa, Beni Halba women have not yet been influenced by the others to establish their own '*Sandoug'*. They have another method of mutual social support. They jointly collect money to support the very poor in the 'cohesive subgroup' to which they belong. A divorced woman from Beni Halba -aged 48 describes the way the women of this ethnic group help each other financially:

"We are all relatives here and we know each others' situations. We know if someone has been sick and is unable to work or when someone dies. We collect money and offer it to the needy person, whether the person is a woman or a man. We are all from one clan here."

'Eliddah' associations are informal property associations whose membership is restricted to women. The vast majority (95 %) of the women respondents are members of 'Iddah' associations, which women migrants established in the 'cohesive subgroup' to which they belong. Women jointly established Eliddah associations with the objective of reducing the burden and inconveniences of collecting utensils from different homes and giving them back when there is an oc-

casion. A shortage of utensils was always noticed after the collection of utensils from each house. This shortage was never redressed. Thus, another objective of these associations is to overcome the shortage encountered when utensils are collected from individual households. In view of this, these associations are established for the benefit of each member. The members keep the utensils in one of their homes whereby each member has the right to use them if she has an occasion and to return them when the occasion is over. In addition to that, women in each settlement jointly use these utensils during religious occasions.

Bargo and Tama women who reside in two different compounds where in each a co-ethnic group living established *'Iddah'* association. A married woman from Bargo, aged 24, explains the way they organised themselves to establish their *'Iddah'* association and keep it functioning, and how they managed it.
"We have one association concerned with house utensils. I was one of the three women who were responsible for the association. We use to work together in the 'Khala' and receive wages and buy 'Eliddah'. We also use to collect 10.000 Sudanese pounds (3) *(= $ 0.04) per month from women in each house and buy 'Iddah'. If someone needs the utensils we give them to her and then she returns them after use."*

Another married woman from Tama, aged 33, describes the way and the purpose for which they established their *'Iddah'* association:
"We contributed money from our wage work and bought 'Eliddah'. Every one of us can use the utensils if she has an occasion such as a death or a wedding."

In Wad Ellaithie, with the exception of women from Fellata and Hausa, all women belonging to the existing ethnic groups (Beni Halba, Misairia, Bargo and Tama) jointly established 'Iddah' association. A divorced woman from Beni Halba, aged 47, describes the origin of the association by explaining its objectives and how members have access to the utensils. Her explanation gives a clue to the 'influence' on these women by those who preceded them in the establishment of the *'Iddah'* association:
"We have 'Iddah' association in which I am a participant. The idea of our 'Iddah' association came about during an occasion that took place in this village. The women recognised the need for 'Eliddah', as one woman was unable to provide all the necessary utensils when she has an occasion. The issue was discussed on that day. Many women from Tama, Bargo, Beni Halba, and Kardafa (Misairia) - participate in this association. Women from Fellata and Hausa do

not participate in our association, because they have their own association. Our association is well organised and we have a woman who is in charge of it. [...] I used to be in charge of this association. Each participant of the association uses 'Eliddah' if she has an occasion."

A married woman from Misairia, aged 42, who stays in Wad Ellaithie explains the problems that the women were experiencing before the establishment of the *'Iddah'* association and how its establishment through women's collectivity has reduced the women's burden:

"I am a participant of the 'Iddah' association. Beni Halba, Bargo, Tama and we, the 'Kardafa' (Misairia,) participate in this association. Before this association was created we used to collect the 'Iddah' for occasions from our relatives and our neighbours. It was not possible to find all that is needed for an occasion. In addition, keeping people's belongings is a big responsibility and very risky, especially if an item is misplaced or broken. [...] The creation of the association has made things easy for us."

Fellata and Hausa have their own separate association, established more than 17 years ago, as one of them told me. The idea of this association came from Fellata and Hausa women in Wad Ellaithie who turned out to be the members of this association. The women collect a fixed monthly amount of money from the members and buy utensils on a monthly basis in addition to those collected. The objectives of this association are similar to those of other *'Iddah'* associations. The keeping and control of the association is the responsibility of the wife of the *'Sheikh'* of Fellata and Hausa who is also a member.

A married woman from Fellata aged 44 who stays in Wad Ellaithie describes how the *'Iddah'* association of Fellata and Hausa is managed:

"I do not participate in the 'Iddah' association of other tribes. We Fellata and Hausa have our own association. The wife of the Sheikh (of Fellata and Hausa) *is responsible for the association. She keeps 'Eliddah in her house and bears the responsibility of giving them out to any woman who has an occasion. She makes sure that the 'Eliddah' are returned to her keeping after such occasions."*

7.4 *'Sandoug'* and *'Iddah'*: new coping strategies for security

The women migrants within their 'cliques' and the 'cohesive subgroup' to which they belong establish their informal associations as a strategy for coping with their insecure living conditions and their daily life struggles. *'Sandoug'* and

'Iddah' are the two major associations that have been identified by this research as one of the decisive mechanisms of women migrants' 'neo-traditional social security'.

'Sandoug'**:** The emergence of the new form of *'Sandoug'* that is brought out by this study is a women's strategy related to their social safety. *'Sandoug'* as a new mechanism of women's security is evident in the women's financial mechanism to support each other as well as the needy in their struggles. It is important to note here that women migrants have no access to formal social security. These constraints induce women to focus on their social networking and subsequently construct their own 'traditional social security'. Hence, these women apply their own strategies aimed at getting funds to establish these savings boxes in order to guarantee the 'traditional' systems of social support. In this view Lachenmann (1997) pointed out that- women bring in their 'traditional' forms of savings clubs, different from the formal savings and credit system, which is considered as too individualistic. Women realize that it is important for them to do something together, to have some common activity. One could call it investing in new security providing relations. In this way, an important security network is constituted (Lachenmann 1997: 57). Owing to scarcity of money, Bargo and Tama women each concentrate on their social networks as important means by which they construct collective actions. This collectivity is evident in the way women take advantage of their wage labour in terms of investment of the return received from their collective wage work in establishing their collective savings boxes and keeping them functioning. In such situation women migrants' *"economic activities complement their relationship network"* (White 1992: 92).

Other women groups e.g. Fellata and Hausa women are influenced by the experience of the Bargo and Tama in establishing their savings boxes. These women establish their savings box with the aim of providing mutual financial assistance in cases of sickness, travel and other circumstances requiring social support. It is noteworthy that they make use of their gatherings for work in the field to set a strategy for establishing *'Sandoug'*. This shows that women's daily presence and meetings in the agricultural fields is used as a means of circulating information among them. It is like reading a daily newspaper about the community. Hence, women migrants' social position as agricultural labour enables them to set strategies for security when meeting at the work place, whilst application of these strategies takes place in the women's private sphere. The linkage which is established between the work sphere and the women's private sphere is an outcome of what is often referred to as 'overlapping' of women's activities with social relations. This structure of 'overlapping' enables women to manoeuvre their own social actions. This is made plausible through exchanging ideas about others' experiences that exert influence on women to set their own coping strategies. This means *"influence may shape the responses and strategies of different actors"* (Long 2001: 19).

From what has been explained, it is evident that the membership of *'Sandoug'* is primarily based on women's belonging to their 'cliques' and the 'cohesive group'. This ensures that ethnic identity matters to women in establishing *'Sandoug'*, which provides women with elements of social support and solidarity. Consequently, this leads to a further argument, which ensures that the personal relationships between the members of *'Sandoug'* as well as the availability of 'trust' are significant elements. The central role of 'trust' in the relationships between women, which is considered as a 'social capital' for them, replaces the institutionalised regulations of the banking systems or formal organizations. The importance of 'trust' lies in the regularity of payments (ref. to Streiffeler and Piszczek 2004: 1) and the obligation of women to participate in the collective work. Another important line of argument is that the objectives of such a *'Sandoug'* show that, *"the material significance of social relationships is very clear"* (White 1992: 93) among co-ethnics. However, women consider their savings boxes to be the main support for the needy – not only financially but also morally (ref. to Lachenmann 1997: 52). This is because the relationships between these women who establish the *'Sandoug'* and the needy and the sick have aspects of solidarity. Therefore, the *'Sandoug'* is a women's coping strategy for security in communities where the focus on social networks is decisive in lessening their social struggles.

'Iddah' associations: These associations are a women's coping strategy with the insecure economic and social conditions that hinder them in the acquisition of these utensils independently in the household. An important line of argument by Lachenmann (1997) suits this situation. The household is too small an institution and its level is too low to guarantee generalised safety and security. The alternative should be systems that are as uncomplicated as possible, which follow participation, power of decision-making, self-administration and self-help (ibid: 59). In view of this, associations formed by women from different households increased the availability of utensils needed by women during occasions and reduced the burden they experienced in the past. The *'Iddah'* associations, therefore, constitute particular resources that women by means of their social networks made available. According to the theory of rational action, women as actors have control over certain resources such as the utensils in which they have interest in keeping as common property and using them in their families and communities' occasions. The 'social capital', therefore constitutes these particular resources, which are the need for the utensils, feeling of a common responsibility, control and common interests of the women migrants. This 'social capital' that is available to the women migrants facilitates their social actions (ref. to Coleman 1988: S98) in terms of women making use of such 'social capital' in establishing the *'Iddah'* associations that constitute an important element of their social security.

It is remarkable that the Fellata and Hausa women who preceded the other women belonging to other ethnic groups living in Wad Ellaithie in the establishment of their utensil's association exert influence on them to establish their own association. What is interesting here is the way these women make use of their social networking despite the ethnic diversity. One could argue that the existence of several ethnic groups of migrants in one compound facilitates women's meeting during the social occasions and the formation of new networks. Certainly, these social occasions are considered as a platform for women's networking. These gatherings encourage women to identify and discuss their social struggles (e.g. the lack of utensils) and to take collective actions to solve them. Thus, these gatherings are considered as a 'social capital' that women use as a resource for taking joint decisions and setting strategies for solving their problems, a reality which binds these women in spite of the ethnic diversity. Furthermore, the joint social action of these groups of women is evidence- which shows that women acquire 'effective agency'. Women from different ethnic groups, according to Kertzer and Madison (1981) generate a tendency towards the construction of collective activities, ignoring ethnic differences to join forces on issues of common concern (Kertzer and Madison 1981: 126). This is made plausible in the collective action of these women, by means of which they managed to overcome the insecure economic conditions and establish *'Iddah'* association. Otherwise, it may be difficult for each group to independently establish its association since these groups are small. This does not only mean a formation of an association but also implies an emergence of new ties between these women. One could argue that the settlement of migrants in clusters restricts the women's mobility and confines their social networks to women belonging to the same ethnic group. It also creates a social distance between women who belong to different ethnic groups. However, the 'clusterability' within one compound results in the emergence of new modes of close relations and new social networking between these women despite the ethnic diversity. Schultz (2005), who studied gender, power, family localization and negotiations of "modernity" in Sudanese households and families, has come to the same conclusion. Constriction of women's mobility creates close relations between women in spite of the diversity in ethnicity and class (Schultz 2005: 212).

7.5 Social networks: a source of women's power and 'agency'

It is important to emphasize that women migrants live in insecure economic conditions. What is, however, most striking is that these constraints induce women to concentrate on their social networks in order to achieve their common goals. Furthermore, one could argue that women take advantage of the resources that are available to them evident in the emergence of new modes of collective actions in the social environment of the Gezira Scheme. These collective actions enable them to establish their informal associations. One could argue that these new modes of collective actions result in the formulation of new networks of relations. Thus, this explains the creativity and ability of women to work with the scarce financial resources by means of these collective actions for collective security and cope with life. Lachenmann (1997), in her study of informal social security in Africa, has come to the same conclusion. Collective work in the fields is often considered as a fundraising source for collective security. The collective fields do constitute an important feature of mutual assistance and a tradition of dependency on social relations (Lachenmann 1997: 52). These findings demonstrate that women as actors acquire 'agency' by means of their social networks which became 'effective' through their collective actions. One needs to refer to the line of argument that says the insecure living conditions induce women to concentrate on their social networks and take advantage of their labour force. This view clarifies on the one hand that there is no clear cut difference between the work sphere and the women's private sphere, which is often referred to as an 'overlapping' of spheres as well as women's activities with their social relations. On the other hand it explains that women's power lies in their social networks, which is evident in their collectivity and, certainly, that women as actors use power to achieve their goals in everyday life. White (1992), who studied gender and class in Bangladesh, has come to the same conclusion. Women's concentration on their networks and relationships as social capital represents the key locus of female power in communities in which networking is the central underlying principle (White 1992: 93). Thus, the concentration of women on their social networks represents the prime means of their power and agency.

Women's associations according to Kertzer and Madison (1981) entail a degree of women's self-governance in terms of the making and enforcing of various obligations applicable to women only (Kertzer and Madison 1981: 125). A suitable example is the *'Iddah'* associations, known to be a women's 'gender specific' common property. This is because, according to the African culture, the preparation of food in social occasions, particularly in the rural areas, is a women's responsibility. This consists of some features of the social structure. Another example is the *'Sandoug'*, as women establish this mainly as a source of financial support for the needy. Further to this are the investments of the return received from collective wage work, a kind of work, which is regarded as a 'gender specific' work for women only. Therefore, independent from men, women migrants as a 'gender category' have the *"capacity to devise ways of coping with life"* (Giddens 1984: 1 – 16). This social reality, which proves that women acquire agency in constructing their 'gendered specific' security, is considered as an addition to Long's thought of an actor-oriented approach.

7.6 Social occasions: within the 'cohesive subgroup'

Social occasions are gatherings of both women and men migrants. In these events 'gender segregation' is seen as the major feature that shapes the outlook of the migrant communities. Such occasions include wedding, death, birth and religious festivals. At these occasions, contribution of money and/or foodstuffs is empirically evident among the vast majority (85 %) of married and unmarried women respondents from all ethnic groups. Women in a single 'cohesive subgroup' (i.e. of the same ethnic group) or in their 'cliques' jointly collect money and foodstuffs to offer at a particular occasion with the aim of helping the family which has the occasion. They also carry out domestic work in the home of the occasion.

In social occasions, particularly weddings, deaths or births, women belonging to the same 'cohesive subgroup' support each other. Women in a single 'cohesive subgroup' jointly provide the host with money and foodstuffs. In such occasions, the execution of domestic work like food preparation is regarded as a women's task. In addition to their participation in the preparation of food at the venue of the occasion, they also prepare food in their homes for the occasion. A

married woman from Tama, aged 38, describes the way Tama women provide social support for each other when there is an occasion in the 'cohesive group':
"If someone dies or gets married women make 'Kissra' in their homes and offer it to the woman who has the occasion. We also cook and wash 'Eliddah' in the home of the occasion until the occasion is over. Yes, we always help each other. We are all here from one clan."
Similar to Tama, Bargo women in a single 'cohesive subgroup' or in their existing 'cliques' provide each other with material and non-material resources during such occasions. A married woman from Bargo, aged 24, relates the way Bargo women in Dar Elsalam camp support each other:
"If there is anything like sickness or death we help each other with money. We offer the money to the person in need who has an occasion, like a poor woman for example, so that she can buy foodstuffs to make 'Karamah'."

Another married woman from Bargo, aged 19, brought up in an urban area in Sudan and moved to Dar Elsalam after her marriage, says:
"The people in this village (i.e. camp) rally round each other. If there is an occasion like death the people cooperate. They collect money and help each other. When the condolencing days are over they also pay the debts incurred by the housekeeper if the person (i.e. the host) has some debts and leave the rest of the money to be spent on latecomers to the occasion. This is what I like."

Beni Halba women offer a more or less similar type of support. A divorced woman from Beni Halba aged 49 explains the way they help each other in occasions:
"I have a strong relationship with the women of Beni Halba because they are our relatives. When there is a wedding we assist each other. We borrow 'Iddah' and beds or whatever we need from the homes of our relative. We also do the work in the home of the occasion. We prepare the food and wash 'Eliddah'. [...] Also if someone dies we provide foodstuffs which the people need at the occasion."

The vast majority (95 %) of the women respondents from Bargo and Tama explain their existing solidarity and 'reciprocity' as a result of their traditional heritage and inherited features. A married woman from Tama, aged 29, demonstrates:
"We are all relatives here and we know everything about each other because everyone of us tells the other if there is anything until we all know. We like to

know each other's problems. For example, we know who is sick or who has given birth so that we can provide food and money. It is our nature to help each other. This is what our elders taught us a long time ago."

In spite of this commonality, a particular case is represented in what a married woman aged 46 states. When she was asked about the source of their reciprocal solidarity, she relates it to the civil war they experienced in Tchad before they migrated:
"We learnt this since the years of war in Tchad; we all help each other."

Social occasions within the 'cohesive subgroup' also include celebrating the religious occasions. The migrant communities targeted by the study are Muslims. Women are active social actors during preparations of the religious occasions and festivities. Since *'Ramadan'* is an important religious occasion for these groups, women migrants undertake joint activities before and during the month of *'Ramadan'*. Most of the women respondents (90 %) assure that they organise special activities as a preparatory process for *'Ramadan'*. Some women jointly contribute money for buying foodstuffs they distribute among themselves to be consumed during *'Ramadan'*. This activity is found particularly among the Bargo who live at the periphery of Elsoreeba village.

Since the preparation of food is a women's task in African culture, women take on the responsibly of preparing special foodstuffs and drinks to be used in this month (i.e. *'Ramadan'*). In Wad Ellaithie, women from the different ethnic groups are organised in an association to carry out these preparations. Some of them call it *'Ramadan'* association while others call it *'Abraih'* (1) association. The members of this association are 30 women from Tama, Beni Halba and Misairia (*'Kardafa'*) whereas each of Fellata and Bargo have their own association. Women gather to prepare *'Abraih'* in each of home of the members. The activity is well organised because each member chooses a day in which women gather at her place. All the members are obliged to bring some foodstuffs for the gathering.
Most (90 %) of the women respondents assert that they gather every day in *'Ramadan'* in small groups within each single 'cohesive subgroup' to break the fasting. These small groups considered as women's 'cliques' usually consist of neighbours, relatives and in-laws. Women participants of each *'clique'* bring their food to break their fasting together in the case of big *'cohesive subgroup'* like Bargo or Tama. Women in small *'cohesive subgroups'* such as Beni Halba,

Fellata and Misairia, break their fasting together. Men belonging to the same 'cohesive subgroup' break their fasting separately from the women. This mostly takes place in the mosque or in the *'Khalwa'* or in the courtyards between the houses, while women eat together inside one of the houses. It is also important to realize that women migrants are in charge of the religious festivities. The following examples demonstrate the women's activities during the religious occasions. A married woman from Beni Halba aged 48 describes the manner in which the women of Beni Halba take their meals, particularly during *'Ramadan'*:

"[...] On normal days we (Beni Halba women) eat separately. Each family eats separately in their home but in 'Ramadan' we women break our fasting together, as you see we are few here. 'Ramadan' is an important month that is why we gather and break our fasting together."

As for Bargo and Tama women, they have similar ways of organising during *'Ramadan'*. Women of these two ethnic groups are predominantly responsible for the religious festivities. This narration by a married woman from Bargo, aged 19, demonstrates women's activities in gatherings during the religious occasions:

"We young women do things together during occasions. For example, in 'Eid' we collect money and buy a goat or a sheep and vegetables. We cook and eat together. We provide the men with food, which they eat in the mosque. This is the way we celebrate the 'Ayad'."

7.7 Social occasions: social support between 'cohesive subgroups'

In general terms, it is empirically evident that even in social occasions there are few contacts between women migrants of different ethnic groups/'cohesive subgroups' in contrast to the ties that exist between women migrants belonging to the same ethnic group. The women of different ethnic groups explicate that their social interactions and mutual social support in social occasions like death and wedding are confined to visits during which they provide each other with foodstuffs and money. This shows the limitation of the social relations between the women of heterogeneous ethnicity, which applies particularly to those who reside in different compounds occupied by co-ethnics.

In Wad Ellaithie, women of the older generation (mothers and grandmothers) from each ethnic group interact collectively to support the women of the other ethnic groups in social occasions. In times of joy or sadness, they jointly offer foodstuffs or money. This is common among the different ethnic groups in this compound. What to collect and how much has to be jointly agreed on by the women associates (of the older generation) in each ethnic group. Beni Halba women explain their social interactions during occasions with women from the other ethnic groups living in this locality as limited to visits in events of joy or sorrow. This is manifested in the joint offers of foodstuffs to the women in charge of the occasion. Women locally identify this form of collectivity and social security *"cooperative"*. This narration from a divorced woman from Beni Halba aged 48 demonstrates the issue:

"We have a good relationship with the people in Wad El Laithie. We are here together and we share with each other the happiness and sadness in this village. We visit Kardafa (Misairia), Tama, Bargo and Hausa only during an occasion. We, the Beni Halba women collect foodstuffs and take to the Bargo and Tama women when they have an occasion. We do not have further relationships with Fellata, Bargo and Tama but we have special cooperation with Kardafa because we work with them in their occasions."

However, this study came across the emergence of a new mode of 'social security' in Wad Ellaithie. Unlike the elder generation, women of the younger generation from the existing heterogeneous ethnic groups build social ties with each other. These unmarried young women work together to help with wedding preparations. However, it is realized that such social support is still stronger among the members of a homogeneous ethnic group compared to those within heterogeneous ethnic groups. It is also evident that young women from all the existing ethnic groups give financial support to the bride or the sister of the groom if the bride is not from the same compound. From amongst themselves, they nominate a woman to collect money and their choice is regardless of the nominee's ethnic identity. Moreover, close friends of the woman getting married provide her with presents. Young men also pursue the same system of financial support whereby they hand the collected money to the groom or to the bride's brother. This form of social support does not exist among the elder generation, who either pay money or offer foodstuffs collected in the zone of the ethnic group.

7.8 Social occasions: women migrants and the *'Arab'*

40 % of women respondents assert that they have social relations with some of the *'Arab'* women, while the remaining 60 % deny any relations with 'Arab' women. The women migrants are not assimilated in the local community or the

'Arab', as the migrants call them. Women migrants do not have considerable social relations as their only contact with the women of the local community is related to work. The *'Arab'* women with whom the women migrants build some sort of social relations are either young women of the same age group, or neighbours of the migrants prior to their move to the camps from local villages. These also include the *'Arab'* women who belong to the families of the partners (sharecroppers) of the women migrants. Very few of these are women tenants who are partners of women migrants or the women migrants and their spouses. These relations are limited to visits during special occasions or, if the women in the tenants' families are in need of some of the agricultural products, the women sharecroppers provide them. A married woman from Tama, aged 38, explains their relations with the *'Arab'* women:
"We only visit women of the 'Arab' whom we know and on special occasions. We provide them with foodstuffs from the products we have, such as Sorghum and also vegetables which we get in lieu of pay when we work during the harvest time."

A married woman from Misairia, aged 42, explains that their relationship with the *'Arab'* is confined to their social contact with the family of their partner:
"We only have relations with our partner's family. We go to them only if there is something related to work or if they have an occasion like condolence or a happy occasion. In such occasions we offer them foodstuffs, which they do not have. In the vegetable harvest season we offer them some of the products which they do not have."

This is a particular case in which a married woman from Misairia aged 40 explains that they have a good relationship with their partners' family. This is the extended family of Wad Ellaithie, the man who established this village and after whom it is named. This family stays at the periphery of Wad Ellaithie where the migrants of heterogeneous ethnic groups reside.
"We have no relations with the 'Arab' women in the nearby villages except with our partner's (tenant's) family with whom we have good relationship. We visit them continuously during occasions and they visit us. We have been partners for several years and they also reside with us here in Wad Ellaithie."
Unlike the previous cases there are some women who have contrary views on the relationship between the 'Arab' and the migrants. They expose the reasons for weak ties between the 'Arab' and the migrants. These three cases prove that some women migrants either have no contacts with the people of the local

community (the 'Arab') or otherwise contacts with them are confined to work relations. A married woman from Tama, aged 28, claims that:
"We do not visit the 'Arabs' whether they have a social occasion or not, but our men go to them for condolences. Why should we visit them when they do not visit us."

Another married woman from Tama aged 35 views the social distance between the *'Arab'* women and them (migrant women) as racial dichotomy.
"We do not have relationships with the 'Arab' women. If the women of our partners need a product we share it with them. When someone dies we go to them for condolences but the 'Arab' women never visit us. I do not know why. Maybe because we are black."

A 30-year-old married woman from Bargo perceives the relation between the *'Arab'* and the migrants as a result of the resources (i.e. land) the Arabs have and of racial difference:
"I am telling you the truth, honestly, the 'Arab' do not help us at all. [...] The 'Arab' women stay at home and do not work in the 'Khala' like us. Since their men have the tenancies, they do not work. They rest in their houses and we are the ones who carry 'Eltouriah'. They do not visit us even if someone here has died. They treat us like this because we are black people. They do not like the black people. They think that they are better than us because they are 'Arab'. We are Muslims but they do not believe or behave as stated in the religion, that we are the same. They do not care about us and that is why their relationship with us is different from the relationship we (i.e. Bargo) *have with each other."*

The following case, which consolidates the previous ones, helps to explain the weak ties between the *'Arab'* and the migrants. It is a statement by a deserted woman from Zagawa[18], aged 29, who stays on the periphery of one of the villages of the local community. She attributes the poor relationship between the *'Arab'* and the migrants to differences in ethnicity and class:
"We do not have relations with our partner or his women other than when we visit them. We also don't visit them unless in urgent matters related to work or when someone is seriously sick or has died. Moreover, we do not have time because we spend most of our time in the 'Khala'. [...] The 'Arab' do not invite us

18 This is the only woman from the Zagawa ethnic group who I interviewed. There are no people from Zagawa found in the localities where the empirical research was conducted other than this woman and her mother and grandmother.

to occasions like weddings because we are not from the same ethnic origin and, of course, they are prosperous and we are not."

7.9 Mutual social support in social occasions versus ethnicity

In social occasions women, particularly co-ethnics are involved in a 'gender specific' joint social activities in terms of *"many social obligations of sharing"* (Lachenmann 1997: 51). They carry out social duties and provide each other with mutual social support, most notably those associated with sadness or sorrow (death and sickness) and occasions of happiness or joy (wedding and giving birth). These duties range from provision of material to non-material resources, which are evident in the undertaking of domestic work, contribution of financial and food resources and provision of moral support. It is important to realise that men do not directly share the benefits that women enjoy in these social occasions.

Mutual social support in social occasions has been found among women belonging to the same ethnic group as well as among women from different ethnic groups. More intense, however, 'social security' is found among co-ethnic women, which is more commonly in terms of mutual social support. This explains, on the one hand, the dependency of co-ethnic women on their social networks. On the other hand, it highlights the feeling of belonging and intimacy among women belonging to the same ethnic group as fact, which proves that ethnic identity matters to the women migrants. The limitation of 'social security' among women belonging to different ethnic groups is clearer among the elder ones whereby their social support is confined to provision of money or foodstuffs in social occasions.

It is important to note here that in the migrant compounds occupied by co-ethnic groups, there appear to be considerable similarities in the ways women interact socially in wedding occasions. However, this is not the case in Wad Ellaithie since several ethnic groups occupy it. In this locality women's ways of interactions and activities in the wedding occasions are connected with their age sets which bring women from different ethnic groups together (ref. to Kertzer and Madison 1981: 125). Evidence shows that in this locality there is an emergence of social change as a result of the construction of a new mode of 'social security' by each of the two gender categories of the younger generation. What concern us more here are women of the younger generation who belong to various ethnic groups as compared to the older women belonging to the same ethnic group. A generational change appeared in the construction of new modes of mutual social support in terms of collective financial and physical support in wedding occasions by women of the younger generation. The younger women use social networking in a wide scope to serve the common goals as compared with women of the older generation. Kertzer and Madison (1981) argue that people of a similar age have certain interests in common as distinct from occupants of other age strata. Thus, age similarity can be the basis of common interest (ibid: 128). Consequently these young women generate a tendency towards the construction of a wide scope of social security across the different cultures, ignoring the differences in ethnic identity.However, despite the emergence of this generational social change, one cannot deny that there still exists intensive mutual social support between the younger women belonging to the same ethnic group. This social reality explains that ethnic identity still matters to women of the younger generation despite the new modes of social change which they generate. Quoting Hamond and Jablow (1976) who have come to the same conclusion; *"Peer relationships that crosscut kin lines do not figure as prominently in women's lives as do links with related women of all ages on the basis of shared responsibilities, joys, and sorrows"* (Hamond and Jablow, 1976: 114 in ibid: 126). It is important to realize that ethnic identity is certainly found to be a matter of importance to the older women. This is evident in the existence of 'ethnic bias' in the construction of 'social security' among older women who belong to the different ethnic groups. This is because women of the older generation belonging to the same ethnic group have intensive mutual social support among themselves compared to that which exists between women from different ethnic groups. Furthermore, in examining the 'gendered social security' among the younger generation belonging to different ethnic groups, utilization of a similar space by the younger men is found to be distinct from that which exists in the younger women's social world. This explains on the one hand the 'gender-specific nature in the construction of collective 'social security' among the younger generation in spite of the ethnic diversity. On the other hand it symbolizes particular cultural changes that the migrant communities are undergoing.

7.10 Religious occasions: a venue for security

'Social security' is also evident in the religious occasions and festivities in which women migrants are social actors. Women through their social networks within their 'cliques' and the 'cohesive subgroup' to which they belong found their way to apply strategies in terms of organising activities for their gatherings in the religious occasions. These gatherings serve as a source of entertainment, which act as social security for women after hard labour in the field. Sharing of food within their 'cliques' in *'Ramadan'* regardless of who brings what demonstrates the existence of this 'social security'. Sharing of money as well as food in the religious occasions and festivities are strategies that women apply within the 'cohesive subgroup' to which they belong. On these grounds, women could fulfil on the one hand the religious values that call for solidarity, sympathy, charity and compassion. On the other hand they could overcome the insecure living conditions, which hinder them from accomplishing these religious values if they act separately.

What is mentioned above proves that ethnic identity matters to the women migrants. Nevertheless, it is evident that women belonging to different ethnic groups get together in a specific period of the year to prepare for *'Ramadan'*. This activity is associated with a religious occasion that brings together all the women despite their ethnic diversity since they are united by one religion i.e. 'Islam'. This coalition shows that women are socially interlocked by religion. Hence, religion can be considered as a 'social capital' that brings women together despite their ethnic diversity and facilitates their mutual social support as well as social solidarity.

7.11 Social inequality

Social inequality evidently exists between the women migrants and the *'Arab'* women. This social inequality hinders frequent social interactions between these two social groups and the assimilation of most women migrants into the sphere of women of the local community. There are different reasons for the women migrants' insights into the existence of this social disparity. Women migrants perceive the "*Arab*" women as a higher class. *"[...] They are prosperous and we are not."* "*[...] They do not work in the field like us. Since their men have the tenancies, they do not work. They are resting inside their houses and we are the ones who carry 'Eltouriah'."*

The women migrants perceive that the *'Arab'* see them as *"black"* or of different ethnic identity. *"[...] The 'Arab' women never visit us. I do not know why.*

*May be because we are black." "They do not visit us even if someone here has died. They treat us like t*his because we are black people." *"The 'Arab' do not invite us for their occasions like wedding because we are not from the same ethnic origin of the 'Arab".*

Aversion of the people of the local community ('the Arab') to the migrants whom they conceive as *"black"*, generate a conception of racial difference, 'ethnic bias' and 'ethnic differentiation'. Thus, class, race and ethnicity as symbols of social difference achieve specific meaning to the women migrants' identity. Consequently, women migrants *"develop boundaries of social group cohesion and social differences between their group and other groups. Identity, ethnicity, gender"* (Santen and Schaafsma 2000: 22) and class are undeniably related. In addition, women migrants see that the *'Arab'* close their eyes to the religious values which assert that human beings are equal regardless of their colour, race or class difference. These, therefore, are reasons that can be cited to explain such social inequality, resulting in little contacts between these two social groups of women. Nevertheless, some women migrants as active social actors are able to build networks of social relations with some of the *'Arab'* women.

Furthermore, it is important to examine the history of the Gezira Scheme in relation to the migrants' settlements. Settlement of the migrants in camps surrounding the villages of the local community is a process of separation that is based on ethnic difference. It is noteworthy that the Sudanese governments, post independence, have pursued the same policy as the British colonial masters in settling the migrants in camps. According to Grätz (2000), who is a German social anthropologist, social and ethnic heterogenisation could be a reaction to different forms of State intervention (Grätz, 2000: 4). Consequently, this policy plays an important role in the non-assimilation of the migrants in the local community and fosters the existence of social inequality between these communities.

7.12 Inter-household relations

There are different forms of social support women migrants provide for each other. These are evident in their activities within the context of inter-household relations (4). Women usually resort to each other and also to male relatives in the instance of borrowing money. Women have many social obligations within the context of inter-household relations. These include caring and performing domestic responsibilities in cases of need, gatherings for eating and coffee and exchanging other material benefits. These social obligations are also evident in the free lodging of new migrants of the same ethnic group and in the hospitality to the guests.

Borrowing and financial support: Borrowing and financial support are done through different channels at various locations. It is found that 50 % of the women respondents rely on their relatives when they need to borrow money. A few of these women resort to their partners when they cannot borrow from their relatives. 40 % of the women respondents receive financial support from their male relatives who work in the cities, while 15 % obtain money from other urban relatives (women and men). 10 % of the women respondents get financial support from female relatives (in the household) who work in the non-farming activities.
Bargo and Tama women assert that they borrow money from their relatives within their 'cohesive subgroups'. They resort to their partners only when they do not find someone to borrow from within the same ethnic group. Men borrow from the male tenants since women do not have direct contact with them. However, empirical evidence shows that there is no single case among Tama women respondents reported on borrowing. Differing from the case of Tama, Bargo women have different channels of borrowing.

A married woman from Bargo aged 24 describes the various channels through which she gets financial support from her urban relatives. She also explains why she does not rely on the tenant:
"I get money from my husband who works in Khartoum and also from my sister who is married and stays in Khartoum. I sometimes also receive money from my brother who works in the same city. I have never tried to borrow from my partner because I do not have that close relationship with the 'Arab'. I ask my relatives if I need something."

Another 24-year-old married woman from Bargo - states to whom she turns to borrow money and how she repays it. Differing from the case of the former, this woman explains the importance of her social relationship with her partner, - a woman tenant, as regards money:
"If I need money I take from my brother, my uncle or the Arab. As my partner is a woman I ask her myself. When I ask her for money she gives it to me. The Arab only helps us by lending us money and we return it as it is agreed upon. I pay the loan to my partner as money or in groundnuts according to our agreement.

The woman whom I share crop with (i.e. a woman tenant) is a kind woman and she lends whenever I ask for a loan."

Borrowing is recognized neither among Fellata and Hausa nor among Misairia. This is because most of Fellata and Hausa women work in the non- non-farming activities. These women cover the financial needs of the others who work in the field. A woman tenant from Fellata (5), aged 44, working in the non-farming activities as well, consolidates this:
"Thank God, we do not need to borrow but as you know, the 'Hawasha' needs a lot of expenses. Thank God, I have this small shop in which I sell breakfast to the 'schoolboys'. That is why I can pay the expenses of the 'Hawasha'. My daughters and their father also work in our 'Hawasha' and one of my daughters works at a big house in 'Khartoum'. The people she works for are very kind to her. This enables us to feed, drink and pay also the expenses of the 'Hawasha'."
Misairia women get financial support from their male relatives who work in the urban areas. A 40-year-old married woman from Misairia says:
"We Misairia women do not borrow money. We receive money from the men. Our husbands and our sons who work in Khartoum give us money."

Women's gatherings for eating: On ordinary days, with the exception of the women of Beni Halba, Fellata and Hausa, women migrants of the same ethnic group who lodge in one compound assure that they all eat together. Women neighbours who are in most cases relatives take their meals together. During *'Ramadan'* women break their fasting together. The women respondents from the different ethnic groups assert that women take their meals in their homes while the men eat in the mosque. A married woman from Bargo, aged 30, asserted that the female relatives and neighbours take their meals together:
"My neighbours are our relatives. We are one family. We eat and drink together. Each brings her food and we gather to eat. We eat a little in the field and when we come back home we also eat together. Women and men eat separately because it is taboo for us to eat together." Women migrants cooperate in order to cope with their social realities in the prevailing social context. As migrants, these women feel the significance of cooperation and reciprocal solidarity. A married woman from Bargo, aged 24, spells out this view and gives a broader picture compared to the previous woman respondent:
"When I moved here I got to know all the people here and my relationship with my cousins became stronger. I assist my neighbours and they also reciprocate. We exchange foodstuffs and gather for coffee, but everyone eats in her home.

We used to eat together, but now it is difficult because of the working days. So, we cooperate with each other, [...] because we live together and we support each in everything. We cooperate and we help each other, we visit each other and we eat and take coffee together. This is very important for me because we are away from home."

Differing from the coherence and solidarity of Bargo and Tama women that are evident for example in their daily sharing of food, Beni Halba women assure that they only share food during *'Ramadan'*. A divorced woman from Beni Halba aged 50 describes the Beni Halba women's daily gatherings for coffee and tea, whereas they only gather for eating in *'Ramadan'*.

"Beni Halba women do not eat in the field and they do not eat with women from the other tribes. They meet daily when they finish their work. They take tea and coffee together and organise daily meetings at all Beni Halba' houses. We only eat together in 'Ramadan'. During Ramadan each one of Beni Halba women brings her food and they all break their fasting together. The Beni Halba men eat together but women do not eat with their men (i.e. their husbands), *as it is a big Taboo."*

Who does domestic work for the needy? Social obligations between women migrants as regards inter-household relations extend to carrying out domestic tasks in cases of need. According to women respondents, these are sickness, childbirth and work in the field. In addition, women are socially obliged to carry out domestic work during the occasions mentioned previously. In cases of need it is mostly women neighbours and relatives who hold these responsibilities. The following examples give a picture that explains the situation where women cooperate with each other in case of need. This explanation by two women highlights a situation of the ethnic groups under study with the exception of Beni Halba. A married woman from Tama, aged 24, explains:

"If you are sick or have given birth, your sister or your sister in-law or women neighbours help you. They cook for you, clean the house, and wash the clothes. Since there is a woman to help, the man does not do the housework. He only does it if there is no woman. It is a big taboo for us if the men do the housework like cooking, but the man can take care of the children if he stays at home and his wife works in the field. Any old woman available or older children of 10 years and above can look after the children. If your neighbour is not going to the field, she can take care of the children until you return from the field. If none

of these people are available, the man (i.e. the husband) *takes care of the children."*

Another picture that shows women's mutual social support in carrying out the domestic tasks in cases of need, is given by a married woman from Bargo aged 30:
"My mother stays with me and sometimes cooks and takes care of the children when I am at work because she does not work in the 'Khala' everyday. If I am sick my women neighbours come and help. They bring us food from their homes and also do the housework. [...] When I go to the 'Khala' I leave my children with this 9 years old girl who is my close relative. She helps me in taking care of the children. Her mother lives in a house behind ours. They are neighbours and relatives."

Differing from the cases of women from the other ethnic groups, it is empirically evident that the social networking is relatively fragmented among the women of Beni Halba. This is made clear in the following experience from a divorced woman from Beni Halba at the age of 50:
"My daughters buy the foodstuffs and cook for us. I take care of the children of my daughters when they work in the 'Khala'. When my daughters and myself work in the 'Khala', we prepare the food for the children and leave them alone at home. When the children were very young, their unmarried aunt who did not work in the 'Khala' used to look after them. If a woman has no one to look after her children, she takes them to the field. If I am sick only my daughters help me at work and at home."

Free lodging of new migrants and guests: New migrants usually lodge in a compound - occupied by the ethnic group to which they belong. Empirical evidence shows that almost all the women respondents agree that women are active in providing the new migrants with free lodging. Old migrants (women and men) provide all possible kind of support for them. Relatives of the new migrants provide them with accommodation until they settle. Men are responsible for helping them build residences in the receiving compound. The women respondents assure that when men preceded women in their migration, they prepare accommodation for their families awaiting to join them. Based on the social context of the migrants in the Gezira Scheme, women and men help the new comers in finding work opportunities. The old women migrants in the compound where the new migrants lodge are socially obliged to serve them with food until they settle. To help them settle these women also share foodstuffs and other household items with them. In addition to that they (the former women migrants) also gather to eat and chat with the new women migrants. According to my observations during the empirical research, relatives who lodge in different places of the Gezira area visit each other. During these visits women are responsible for the hospitality of the guests until they leave. These are the ways the women respondents from different ethnic groups explain how they provide the new migrants and the guests with lodgings and material goods.

A 30-year-old married woman from Tama gives a complete picture of the hospitality and lodging of the new migrants:

"When there are women guests in one of the homes, we (women) *offer the guests food until they leave. All women in the village come together to eat with the women guests at the host's residence. They bring food, coffee or tea. They eat, take coffee and tea and chat with the guests. If there are people from our tribe who came to look for work, they stay with their relatives until they build a house. Women here cook for them and provide them with some household belongings. Both women and men give them money, sugar and foodstuffs like Sorghum which were leftovers from the previous season."*

A married woman from Bargo, aged 24, asserts that Bargo women provide hospitality only for guests from the same ethnic group:

"If there is a female guest, the women bring food, coffee and tea. We eat, drink coffee and chat together in the home of the host. We do this only here in our village but not for others."

A divorced woman from Beni Halba aged 47 clarifies the different activities that are carried out by the old migrants (women and men) in order to support the new migrants until they settle:

"The newcomers from Beni Halba stay with us in one of the houses until the men build a place for them to stay. Women of Beni Halba prepare food, tea and coffee for them. The people of the whole tribe here gather every day to eat with the newcomers until they settle. The old people (former migrants) *from Beni Halba search for work opportunities for them. They introduce them to the tenants who need people for crop sharing or whom they want to sublease land."*

In a way different from what was explained by the previous women respondents, another woman from Beni Halba, divorced, and aged 50, highlights the way she settled:

"When I moved here my daughter helped me fetch water to build my house. I paid a wage labourer from Fellata to build my house. My brother Ali is the only one who helped me build the house."

The following narration by a 61-year-old married woman from Hausa concerns the welcoming of guests and the lodging of the new migrants from Fellata and Hausa ethnic groups. Provision of these services in the case of Fellata and Hausa is based on the women's status and age. On these bases there are divisions of social obligations where married and elder women have responsibilities that are different from the young unmarried women. However, the social interactions between women from heterogeneous ethnic groups in Wad Ellaithie in the presence of guests/new migrants are in the form of exchange of visits that are limited to taking coffee once with them.

"When new migrants arrive from Fellata or Hausa, we provide the newcomers with food, coffee and tea for seven days and support them to stay. We help them build their houses or give them money. The women cook for them and provide them with household belongings until they settle. In presence of guests among Fellata and Hausa, married women and old women gather for 7 days to eat and take coffee. Young women go only for coffee because they are busy with working in the field. But in the presence of guests among the other tribes we only take coffee once. Women from the other tribes (Bargo, Tama, Kardafa and Beni Halba) also only visit our guests once to take coffee with them."

7.13 'Social security' in the context of inter-household relations

Inter-household relations involve traditional relations such as kin and neighbourhood, which are considered the social resources of the women migrants. The inter-household relations constitute important means of 'social security' for the women migrants. They take advantage of the inter-household relations to operate several social obligations of sharing and social support. In cases of need, women fulfil the needs of their households and work responsibilities by calling on the social support networks of inter-household relationships. Women's social obligations and social support are represented in different forms and through different means of social resources.

Money lending: Borrowing from relatives is common among women migrants in times of crises. It is not only because *"women in general are less creditworthy"* Lachenmann (1997: 52), but also because women migrants have no access to credit. Nevertheless, by taking advantage of the available 'social capital', women can compensate for this by borrowing from relatives. Thus, money lending within the same ethnic group is arranged to avoid getting money from outside. Women migrants make use of the *"advantage of 'traditional' social relations"* (Lachenmann 1997: 52) within the same ethnic group to which they belong. For getting along in cases of need, women - resort firstly to their close relatives, either women or men, or other co-ethnics on whom they can rely to lend them money. In the second place, they turn to their partners with whom the relationship is only considered as one of work. This is attributed to the fact that kin relations are essential in providing access to a given network. Kin relations appear to tremendously reduce risk in networks with lending activities due to the availability of strong ties and high level of trust (Kasarjyan and Kroff 2006: 28). Likewise Lachenmann (1997) asserts; it is difficult to step out of the ethnic group relations because they guarantee survival, which no other relation does. (Lachenmann 1997: 52). This explains that kin relations are considered as a key part of the social resources of women. Another following line of argument maintains this finding. Although this study has evidently maintained the importance of physical closeness in supportive relations, it is to emphasize that kin relations remain the key factor in provision of social support even if those relatives are not reachable. This is evident in the financial support that women migrants in the Gezira Scheme get from their urban relatives.

It has been found that borrowed money is most commonly used for cultivation, the buying of foodstuffs and funeral expenses. On the one hand, this shows that *"the material significance of social relationships is very clear"* (White 1992: 93). On the other hand, it illustrates that, as Lachenmann (1997) writes, moneylenders are very important to social and productive security. They are often not (only) usurers, but represent important safety networks for women, as well as personal dependence. They still provide food when somebody is starving before the harvest (Lachenmann 1997: 52).

Domestic responsibilities: Domestic responsibilities are considered as an important social obligation that women operate in the context of inter-household relations. They include different household activities like the preparation of food and the care of children. In their everyday life women migrants usually resort to close relatives and to people with whom the social relations are built on free choice, for example friends and neighbours (Platte: 2000: 208). It is evident that domestic work is not a household private sphere in time of crisis or need. It is a 'gender specific' responsibility of women of the neighbourhood who are in most cases close relatives, in-laws or neighbours. Thus, women's traditional relations are social resources that women use to carry out domestic responsibilities for the sick and those who have given birth plus the care of their children. Taking care of children while some women are still working in the field is the responsibility of the elder children and the old women who do not work in the field anymore. Quoting Padmanabhan (2002) *"Interhousehold co-operations may be of voluntary nature, but often follow social obligations and have to bridge differences in age and status"* (Padmanabhan 2002: 149).

In view of the facts explained above, social obligations and the sharing of responsibilities are available in terms of the mutual social support that women provide in the context of their 'clique/(s)' in which women are combined by means of their traditional social relations. Women take *advantage of their traditional relations"* (Lachenmann 1997: 52) as a 'social capital' in which 'trust' is a significant element. Women's trustworthiness and reliability on each other emanate from their belonging to their 'cliques' and the 'cohesive subgroup', the properties of which bind them together. This again proves that the issue of ethnicity matters to the women migrants. One could argue that social networks of women that build on ethnic relations are durable obligations that last for one's entire life. According to Scott (1991) 'durability' means how enduring the underlying relations and obligations are, when activated in particular connections. The relations constantly activated in interaction are highly durable (Scott 1991: 32).

It is evident that women migrants live in a bound social set-up about which some of them perceive the way of social life in the migrant camps as consolation for being away from home. *"[...] We cooperate with each other...[...]...and because we live together and we support each other by food and everything. We cooperate and help each other, we visit each other and eat and take coffee together, this is very important for me because we are away from home"*. Hence, as Roth & Speranza (2000) noted, bilateral relatives and other traditional relations constitute networks for daily activities and are necessary in crisis situations (ibid). Another important line of argument that suits this situation is: *"It is not the networks per se that are important but the meanings these networks hold for their members and possibilities for collective action and personal benefit that they open"* (Krishna and Uphoff 2002: 100).

Free lodging of new migrants and guests: Lodging of new migrants and guests is a gender division of labour between - former migrants who belong to the same ethnic group. Several social obligations towards the newcomers are divided between the two gender categories. However, in these kinds of 'coping capacity', it is predominantly women who contribute. Similarly, Lachenmann writes *"care, as an important element of social security mainly provided by women, is made available"* for persons in need – over and above reproduction work – mainly done by women (Lachenmann 1997: 50 - 51). It is important to realize that the activities in which women engage to lodge the new migrants not only demonstrate the gender division of labour but they maintain the 'gender specific' 'social security' as well. The presence of new migrants is a room for provision of 'social security' that is manifest in different forms of social support and social solidarity which facilitate their coping with life in the receiving context. In addition to that, women's gatherings in the presence of the new migrants and guests are not only considered as sharing of material goods. These gatherings are also entertainment for the newcomers and the former women migrants after hard work in the field. Furthermore, these gathering serve as venues where women chat and disseminate news about the community back home as well as the diffusion of information (e.g. about the receiving context) to the newcomers.

7.14 Types of relations and formation of women's 'cliques'

The particular types of social networks of relations in the women migrants' private sphere are 'multiplex' as they involve combination of a variety of significantly distinctive relations. They form a partial network in which ethnic, kin, inlaws, neighbourly and friendship relations combined into a single, multistandard relationship. Women employ these traditional social ties to form their own 'cliques' within each 'cohesive subgroup'. The properties of the 'cohesive subgroup' also combine the women together in their 'cliques'. *"Most of the active and even intimate network members"* (Wellman 1992: 217) with whom women socialize are the members of their 'clique'. Women's relationships within their 'cliques' are a key part of their social resources. They are an important means by which they exchange material and non-material resources. For example, the gathering of the clique's members on daily basis for sharing of food is considered an important element of security. These gatherings provide a forum for entertainment and a venue for chatting and gossiping and also a platform for circulating information in the community. The women gatherings also increase their degree of intimacy in terms of awareness of each other's problems, and how they organise themselves to find solutions for these problems.

This is manifest in cases such as sickness of a 'clique' member, or birth, or any problem that excludes her from doing the domestic work and from going to the field. Thus, in cases of need the 'clique' members are the same group of women who carry out the domestic work as well as the work in the field (e.g. *'Musaada'*). Such 'overlapping' of activities with social relations provide empirical evidence which shows that women's 'cliques' are an important resource in their social life. Therefore, the women's 'cliques' as 'social capital' constitute their social structure and facilitate their social actions and consequently considered means of women's social power.

7.15 'Social capital'

The women migrants under study acquire various forms of 'social capital'. Each form is defined by its function (Coleman 1988: S99). The women migrants' 'clique' is a small homogeneous group. This homogeneity emanates from the sharing of common properties and traditional relations (ref. to Buchenrieder and Dufhues 2006: 28). In their 'cliques', women migrants are bound by their traditional relations and 'intimate social circles' such as neighbourly relations and kin relations. The prevalence of these relations amongst each clique's members illustrates that these women share more frequent interactions between each other. This demonstrates the availability of the 'bonding social capital' (ref. to Gittel and Vidal, 1998 and Lin 1982 in Buchenrieder 2006: 8). Thus, these traditional relations constitute 'bonding social capital' which facilitates social sharing e.g. the sharing of food and other material items and of information. It also brings about social obligations e.g. holding the responsibility of domestic work in times of need. One could argue that to achieve their own goals, women foster good relations with their clique's members to build up their 'social capital'.

Women from different ethnic groups' establish informal structural arrangements. These two empirical examples illustrate these arrangements in terms of women's social networks that facilitate their collective actions and in turn constitute 'structural social capital'. 1/ The same age of folks of the younger generation that facilitates their collective sharing and mutually beneficial action in wedding occasions despite their different ethnic identity; 2/ the religious values that bind women and integrate them together despite their ethnic diversity to undertake collective activities and share material goods. Buchenrieder (2006) in the following argument accords with this situation; 'structural social capital' binds individuals in groups to each other and bridges divisions between ethnic and societal groups, which may lead to social inclusion. Furthermore, these collective actions originate from the women's *"cognitive social capital"* (Buchenrieder 2006: 10). With reference to the two empirical examples mentioned, this form of 'social capital' is demonstrated by: the same age of folks of the young generation and the religious values. These empirical examples proves that the *"'structural' and 'cognitive social capital' can be complementary"* (Buchenrieder 2006: 10).

It is also important to realize that belonging to the same ethnic group brings about concrete networks of relations. These networks are vital in generating trust, which in turn is considered as a key element of 'social capital'. Elements of 'social capital' vary but tend to centre on trust relationships that facilitate women's social actions. Common rules and norms pertaining to 'reciprocity' and mutual help are expected to build trust and connectedness among women (ref. to Bryceson 2000). In view of this, 'social capital' facilitates women's social actions and *"[...] productive activity. For example, a group within which there is extensive trustworthiness and extensive trust is able to accomplish much more than a comparable group without that trustworthiness and trust"* (Coleman 1988: S99 - S100). Women as social actors employ the 'social capital' that is available to them as a foundation for the construction of their 'social security' and, consequently, for reaching their common goals. Another important line of argument is that utilization of the available 'social capital' by women migrants means, as Giddens (1984) postulates, that women are knowledgeable and capable as social actors to monitor their own actions, to solve their problems and to intervene in the flow of social events around them (Giddens 1984: 1 – 16). The theoretical interpretation of the women's social actions embrace, in addition to the 'knowledgeability' and 'capability', other resources such as 'feeling, emotions, and identities (Turner 1992: 91 in Long 2001: 18). It is important to note here, that these resources represent part of the properties that women migrants share. The properties that women share as members of their own 'clique' or the 'cohesive subgroup' to which they belong are considered as constituents of their social networks. These properties offer them (women) 'social capital'. These properties are represented in: 1/ ethnocentricity (i.e. assimilation in the same ethnic group), 2/ belonging to one region of origin, which generate mutuality of ties, 3/ binding by the traditional relations, 4/ the feeling of intimacy, 5/ operating similar forms of labor, 6/ acquirement of no resources other than their human resource, 7/ sharing the rural destiny and, 8/ reachability and closeness is an important property because women in their 'cliques' or the 'cohesive subgroup', as Scott (1991) contends, can easily contact one another through a limited number of steps (Scott 1991: 32). The fact that the migrant communities are settled in clusters based on ethnic grouping enables this connection to take place. However, the empirical evidence in the research locality occupied by various ethnic groups proves another line of argument. Provision of goods and services as an important kind of social support is positively related to physical access, either through frequent contact or residential proximity. Physical access enables network members to deliver services even when their relationship is not strong (Wellman 1992: 221). Furthermore, these properties generate frequent contact and 'overlapping' of relations and encourage the provision of mutual social support in terms of material and non-material resources. This social support is, on the one hand, evident in encouraging reciprocal rounds of support, sharing of food and other material goods and facilitating construction of informal financial support. On the other hand it is evident in fostering shared values, increasing mutual awareness of needs and resources, exchanging of information between women and, mitigating the feeling of being away from home (ref. to: ibid.).

Therefore, women migrants' social realities enable them to be bound to each other whereby the resources they share are considered as a 'social capital'. This 'social capital' constitutes the women migrants' social structure and facilitates their social actions (ref. to Coleman 1988: S98). Thus women, as Long (1992) argues, are actively engaged in the construction of their own social worlds (Long 1992: 24) in which they establish a 'coping capacity' and a network of social safety.

It is important to emphasize that since social networks and 'social capital' have not featured in the discussion of rural Sudan, a social capital approach is particularly vital for further social research.

7.16 Conclusion

From what has been explained, it becomes clear that construction of 'traditional social security' represents a cornerstone in the cultural constitution of women migrants. Women's building of their own social world enables them to construct 'gender specific' social networks parallel to that of men. Consequently, they are able to construct their own 'neo-traditional' saving systems, *'Iddah'* associations, etc. *"for securing their livelihood"* (Lachenmann 1997: 57). However, it is important to realize that these activities should not only be considered as economic but they also bring about socio-cultural parameters. In addition, as Lachenmann (1997) contends, these activities create important space for the symbolic and spiritual strengthening of coping forces (ibid: 51). One could argue that this is certainly very significant for these women who, on the one hand, are experiencing cultural discourses that are held responsible for the segregation between the two gender categories. On the other hand, they live in a disadvantageous position where they have no access to 'formal social security'. What is, however, most striking is that these constraints induce women to realize the significance of their own social networks, which are *"evidently important to their own female identity"* (ibid: 57). Thus, by means of their social networks women migrants develop a collective identity and common forms of organising. This is made plausible through their collective actions in institutionalisation of their informal associations. Moghadam (2005) who has a similar line of argument writes; a collective identity ensures alliances and cooperation across women's social networks (Moghadam 2005:92). For example, women encounter various problems in their private sphere that induce them to construct collective actions. Money is one of the scarcest resources in the migrant localities. To manage such struggles, new dimensions of actors' strategies emerge at the work sphere of the receiving context – the Gezira Scheme – by means of social networks of the women migrants and, consequently, they achieve their common goals. Likewise Lachenmann (1997) reveals that women peasants through their large membership are able to guarantee a certain social stability and establish new safety nets in a society characterised by impoverishment (Lachenmann 1997: 57). Schultz (2005) pointed out that women are inventive through institutionalisation of mutual help to achieve cooperation within their community (Schultz 2005: 211). Thus, by means of their collective actions, strategies, mutual social support and social obligations that form a foundation of women migrants' safety nets, women are found to be bound by several social ties. According to Kabeer (1992), in reality, all labour activities can be referred to as different kinds of relationships between the different social actors involved. Therefore, different networks include patron-client relations, inter-household organizations, neighbourhood networks, kinship and lineage relations or work groups and social action groups (Kabeer 1992: 10 - 11). Furthermore, social activities and strategies, as Lachenmann (1997) pointed out, are embedded in a system of solidarity, kin relations, peer-groups (Lachenmann 1997: 50), neighbourly relations and inter-household relations.

Joint activities are evidence of what is often referred to as an 'overlapping' of women's activities with their social relations. It is also evident that the forms of 'social capital' that are available to the women migrants are key elements in the fulfilment of their 'social security'. Women's construction of their 'social security' shows the material as well as non-material significance of their social networks. Furthermore, this social system generated by women migrants has maintained solidarity and 'reciprocity' not only among women belonging to the same ethnic group but also between women of heterogeneous ethnic identities. Hence, social networks among women migrants are highly decisive in the fulfilment of their 'social security'. This signifies as White (1992) asserts, that women's social networks constitute their chief resources (White 1992: 88) and centre of power.

Notes

(1) *'Abraih'* is a special drink of *'Ramadan'*. It is made of Sorghum and spices. Its preparation, which is regarded as women's work, takes approximately one week. The last day of preparation requires baking the paste. Women gather in each house to do the baking. The baked-paste is stored dry. In time of need it is soaked in water and ready for drinking.

(2) '*Sandoug'* is known among the African women in terms of a rotating savings box, which women establish with an economic objective. Thus, it is considered as a women's informal association. For running such a savings box women nominate one of the members as a keeper of the box. The members of *'Sandoug'* are usually relatives, neighbours and friends. Every month the members pay a fixed sum of money to the '*Sandoug'* keeper who, in turn, gives the monthly total to one of the members according to the sequence of payment agreed by the group.

(3) Meant here is the Sudanese pound the available currency during the fieldwork of this study, where one Sudanese Dinar = 10 Sudanese Pound and, 280 Sudanese Dinar (i.e. 2800 Sudanese Pound) = 1 Euro.

(4) Some of the empirical data on these activities are based on my observations.

(5) Fellata and Hausa who can become tenants belong predominately to the second generation of these migrants who could obtain Sudanese nationality. According to the Gezira Scheme regulations the tenancies should be given to those who are Sudanese by nationality.

8. Social isolation within the 'cohesive subgroup': case studies

Noora

"You do not know Noora? You have not met her yet. She knows everything and will tell you about many things. She is not like us."

8.1 Getting to know the unique case

In the third week of my empirical research in the first locality and at the end of one of my long fieldwork days after the sunset, I was leaving a camp of Bargo accompanied by two women from the camp, my counterpart and her cousin. When we reached a small courtyard on our way to the periphery of the camp, the cousin of my counterpart asked me whether I had interviewed Noora, pointing at her house. When I said no, my counterpart said: *"You do not know Noora? You have not met her yet. She knows everything and will tell you about many things. She is not like us"*. These words struck me and I became eager to know who Noora was and what made her different from the other women in the camp. Despite my eagerness to know from that moment on I chose to save my questions for Noora, not wanting my counterpart and her cousin's answers to influence my reaction to Noora herself. Impelled by my curiosity I asked my counterpart if we could now call on Noora to meet her and request an appointment for an interview.

Since these two women accompanied me I did not need permission to enter Noora's house. On entering, I saw a woman making coffee in the house yard and two men who, I discovered later, were Noor's husband and father in-law. I could not see her features in the darkness, despite the kerosene lamp (Fanoos) that she was using. All I could distinguish at that moment was her strong voice, her friendly welcome and her good Arabic accent. In accordance with my knowledge of local cultural discourse I first directed my attention to the two men and explained to them the purpose of my visit to the camp, even though I was aware of their knowledge of it. The old man (Noora's father in-law) accepted my request to interview Noora, while her husband maintained his silence. I learned the following day that Noora had agreed to be interviewed at the house of one of her neighbours, a woman who I had already interviewed. I agreed to conduct the interview outside Noora's house despite my knowledge as a researcher that the best place would be the interviewee's house. We met there and, after we took coffee together with two of her neighbours and chatted with the women, I asked Noora whether she would like to be interviewed alone. She preferred to be interviewed in the presence of her neighbours. I could also see the willingness in the eyes of Noora's neighbours to attend the interview. I was afraid that they would affect the interview and spoil my plan to find out about Noora from her alone. Fortunately, they were content just to listen, a situation aided by Noora's personality. She was not only a talkative and a powerful woman in comparison with her neighbours but also came to the point very quickly.

Noora is a young married woman from Bargo, aged 19. Her father, who came from Tchad to teach Qur'an and to work in Sudan, returned to Chad when she was a child at the age of 4. He left them (her mother, herself and her sisters and brothers) in a city in the mid of the Sudan and since that time he has had no contact with them. She is a unique case among the women belonging to the same ethnic group in this camp. Her uniqueness stems from being brought up in a city. Her urban style gave her the knowledge and the opportunity to be the only educated woman in the camp.

8.2 Looking for the relatives: reconstruction of social networks between kinfolk

Noora's distinctiveness among the other women in her current settlement boosts my interest to know more and more about her case. One question was enough to prompt a detailed answer. On asking her when she moved from the city and settle in the camp in the Gezira area, she answered:

"When I was 14 years old, I asked my mum about my father and his relatives and she told me to go and ask an old man living in the city (where she was brought up) who knows better about old fellows. So, I went and asked him. He told me that I have an uncle here in the Gezira, in X-village who came from Tchad to look for his brother, my father, but he assured me that my father was not there with my uncle. My uncle's sons also came to look for their father. They all then stayed here. So, I came here alone and I kept on asking the people here about my uncle until I found him. I asked him about my father but he said that he hasn't known anything about him for a long time, as when he left for Tchad, he did not tell him. He also told me that he knows my father has sons and daughters but he does not know where they are! So, in this way I got to know my father's relatives. So I stayed here. I also found my aunt and married my uncle's son (i.e.

her cousin). They all went back with me to meet my mother and we had the wedding there. Then I stayed here in X-village".

Noora's particularity is evident in several aspects. She is the only educated woman among the women of Bargo, at least in the localities of the fieldwork. Being brought up in an urban area away from her kin and / ethnic group resulted in her distinctiveness from the other women migrants belonging to the Bargo ethnic group. It is necessary to consider the effect of these aspects on her personality and behaviour, which is evident in the action she has taken to look for her relatives and in the way she has chosen to construct social networks between kinfolk. This action explains, on the one hand, her realization of the importance of the construction of social networks among the same kin at a very young age. On the other hand it explicates the enormous difference between her and the other women migrants belonging to the same ethnic group. Her urban life style has provided her with the ability to move on her own, whilst the other women's mobility is restricted by the available traditional and cultural discourse. It is remarkable that the Bargo women's mobility is characterised by a lack of geographical mobility. Their mobility is restricted to the neighbourhood where they move in groups. Moreover, unmarried women have more limited space in their mobility as compared to married ones.

8.3 Gender relations: facing husband's hegemony – a constraint for sharing knowledge and narrowing social distance

An hour into the interview we heard a man calling Noora. I could only see his head over 'Elsareef'. I knew that this was Noora's husband. I asked Noora whether he knew she was here and she said yes. Then I ventured to ask him to let her stay a little longer as we were approaching the end of the meeting. He replied angrily, stating:

"I have no time, we should go to work. I have nothing to do with the other women I am only responsible for my right."

With the phrase *"my right"*, he was referring to Noora, his wife. I told him I accepted what he said, thanked him and released Noora immediately. She whispered to me while she was leaving:

"Hey, do not listen to what he is saying, I will come to you another day to continue the interview because I am interested in this discussion." After four days she returned to continue the interview at her neighbour's home and that one went well. She also participated in one of the group discussions. In my second interview with her, she told me about her studies and social activities while she was in the city, how she enjoys studying the Qur'an, how her residence in the

camp has stopped her continuing her studies and how much she would like to continue them. In her first months in the camp she assembled the women at her place in order to teach them the Qur'an but unfortunately she could not continue. She says:

"When I came here at first I used to gather the women and teach them how to read the Qur'an, but after a while my husband objected to our meeting and studying at my house. He simply forbade it. I am really looking forward to finishing my studies and I am really looking for someone to teach me. I want to finish my studies and find a good job. I am thinking seriously of finding a way out to fulfil my interest. The work here is hard and I do not want my children to work in the field".

Despite her short time stay within her ethnic group, Noora as a social actor has gathered knowledge about the social reality of this group as well as about the social difference between her and the women in the camp. She has tried not to give in to the feeling of social isolation. Instead, she has processed this knowledge to construct a different meaning for this social field through her new social networks by sharing her religious knowledge with the women. Another line of argument is that she has tried to take advantage of the social networks of the women in the camp while shaping and transforming them to her own interests i.e. the teaching of the Qur'an.

Noora is facing a patriarchal culture, evident in the hegemony of the husband. She is trapped in the cycle of her kin structures (ref. to Thieme 2006:196). Her husband's attempt to control her emanates from the fact that *"men fear their non-conformity with the patriarchal institution of marriage and the values and norms that go along with this institution"* (Santen & Schaafsma 2000: 52). If women as social actors are allowed by the exiting gender ideology to freely constructing their private sphere *"men are negatively sanctioned for interfering"* (Nageeb 2004: 186) in this sphere. The traditional male authority and the social and gender order has structured the (undeniable) social isolation of women within the community of their ethnic origin. *"This is not to argue that women are passively subjected to these frontiers"* (ibid.). Instead, as Noora's case shows *" Hey, do not listen to what he is saying, I will come to you another day to continue the interview because I am interested in this discussion."* She also says: *"I am thinking seriously of finding a way out to fulfil my interest."* Thus, these statements show that by applying their own strategies, women as actors could escape the traditional male authority over women. Likewise, Santen and

Schaafsma (2000) argue that women easily escape the patriarchal structure of their societies in order to fulfil their own interest (Santen & Schaafsma 2000: 52). It is to emphasize that the women as social actors are capable and knowledgeable of the way they construct their own social networks in which power is embedded. According to Nageeb (2004) in her writing on women's private space, the social guardianship through traditional male authority on women's private spaces should not be perceived merely as control. Instead, a deeper meaning of guardianship lies in the way it reveals the embeddedness of women's private spaces in a social system and structure (Nageeb 2004: 186).

8.4 Social isolation: comparing urban and traditional rural life

This case shows that it is rather difficult for a young woman from Bargo who has been brought up outside the migrants' communities to be integrated and engaged in their way of life. When Noora was asked how she felt about her movement to the camp and whether she liked the way of life:

"No, I would like to go back to the city and stay there with my relatives. There our land is fertile, we have mangos, oranges and the water of the Nile. There we used to go and have fun, but here we just work, nothing more. There we had the women committee, we used to gather, attend lectures and meet to discuss our problems. We had many social activities; we study together, read the Qur'an and do many other things beside work. Here honestly I couldn't adapt myself. I got to know people and I visit my neighbours, but I work most of the time and we walk for a long distance to fetch the water". She continued: "Yes, here I know a lot of people but not with the same intimacy. They visit each other, they help each other and this is what I like, but if I am sick only my neighbours help me. We, Nagat, Nadia and I (Noora and her neighbours), *stand together. We cook together sometimes.*

One could argue that although Noora's migration is characterised by kin affiliations and by changing of social status, her settlement in the migrants' community provides her with mixed feelings. The reallocation to a new place signifies physical displacement but the feeling of being out of place signifies mental displacement in which the individual identity is challenged. However, in analysing her case, one has to examine why Noora is rejecting her new life style. She is a special and unique case in that she has acquired different social values and a different nature of identity from that of being brought up in an urban area in the absence of a father (from Bargo), which gave her the power to reject the social values of her kinfolk. The feeling of social isolation she is currently experiencing is grounded in a mode of social distance between her as an educated woman and the women of her respective ethnic group who are illiterate. Another factor is the aversion of these women to her due to her mother belonging to a different clan from theirs. Another cause of Noora's isolation is the loss of the urban social life as a means of enjoyment, access to education and institutionalised social activities and of fulfilling aspirations to a higher social position. The absence of these advantages and the fear of not fulfilling her goals, in addition to the drastic difference between urban and traditional rural life of overwhelming hard work in the field, made her doubtful of staying among her respective ethnic group. Furthermore, it created a feeling of social isolation and a loss of identity, resulting in a dream of returning to the urban area in order to achieve her goals. Nevertheless, she does not deny the advantage of living among the people of her respective ethnic group, combined by their 'bonding social capital' and thus living in a bound social set-up full of solidarity. In spite of these facts she only managed to construct her social networks among her neighbours. It is important to note that Noora's two neighbours are in a similar social position to her. They are Bargo women who have been brought up in an urban area and moved with their husbands to the Gezira area. Evidence shows that these women form their own 'clique' because they are socially isolated from most of the women of their respective ethnic group.

Safia

"I am really affected by the way of life that I am experiencing with them. ...There are many differences between me and these people and this is what I do not like at all."

8.5 Getting to know each other

Approaching one of the research localities, a Bargo camp which lies along a minor canal of the GS, one notices that there are three houses at the periphery of the village, a noticeable distance away from the others. This is normal in the villages of the local community where there are many yards between the houses of the migrants on the periphery of the village and those of the local community. However, it is a questionable matter in a migrant camp such as Bargo, in which inhabitants belong to same ethnic group. In my first days in this camp I discovered that the first of the three houses was Safia's house. I asked my counterpart to introduce me to Safia. On entering her place I saw a slim and relatively short young woman with a bright colour in comparison to the other women I met in this camp. She seemed tired when she met us. She had just come back from the field. Since every woman in the camp knows of my presence it does not take me long to introduce myself and my research aims and to make an appointment to interview her in the coming days. Contrary to my impression on first meeting her, she is a talkative woman. Her answers to my questions were in the form of long stories which, despite my wealth of experience in conducting interviews, made it difficult to move on to other issues.

Safia is a married woman from Bargo aged 25. Her husband belongs to the Bargo *'Selaihab'*. She has two daughters; the eldest is three years old and the younger one is 18 months. Her maternal and paternal grandparents migrated from Tchad and stayed in a suburb of one of the big cities in the middle of Sudan (outside the Gezira Scheme). Her parents were born and married in this suburb. They belong to the Bargo ethnic group but from two different clans.

"My father is from the Bargo 'Selaihab' like my husband but my mother is Bargo 'Maimawia'". They died when she was a child. *"I am an orphan. My father and my mother died when I was a child. My sisters brought me up. They took care of me until they married me to my husband."*
Safia, like Noora was not raised among her respective ethnic group in the Gezira area but in the above-mentioned suburb, the destination of her grandparents.

8.6 Movement to the Gezira: living among respective ethnic group

"My husband saw me at the wedding of one of my friend's. We are from the same tribe, Bargo, but not relatives. After two years of marriage and after I gave birth to my eldest daughter my husband asked me to move with him to the Gezira to stay with his mother because he is her only son who stays with her. I agreed and moved with him to this village (a camp of Bargo in the Gezira scheme) *but before my move I did not know anything about this place or anyone here. In my first year here I stayed in the house of my husband and his mother (whom I call 'my aunt' as a matter of respect) and we used to work together in the 'Khala'. But when his brother* (i.e. Safia's brother in-law) *brought his wife problems began to occur. We all used to stay in the same house. I used to be nice to her. For example when she organized 'Nafeer' I used to help cook for the 'Nafeer' people and prepare drinking water and tea. In spite of this she still made life difficult for me as I was a stranger in their family. She is a relative of my husband's mother. One day we had a big quarrel but unfortunately, my aunt* (mother in-law) *sided with her. I really felt that I am a stranger among them and I was upset because I felt lonely. Men interfered since they are responsible for us and advise us. They said to us that we have to respect ourselves and - take care of our children otherwise they would send us back to our families after they cut our tongues.... After sometime, I moved with my husband to this house... In fact, we were the only women who had clashes since I moved to this place and this is because I am away from my relatives and a stranger in this place."*

In talking about her in-laws, Safia also explains the lack of their social support and the quality of their social relations with her relatives:

"The people here do not even care about helping me... Even my husband's sisters (sisters in-law) *do not help me. I am surprised and even asked them why but I did not get an answer."*

She continues:

"My husband's relatives have no contact with my relatives because whenever a person dies in my family they do not bother themselves to go with me. When my sister died my relatives asked me about them. I said to them I couldn't force them. They just have relations with their relatives and the people who are here in this village."

When she was asked about her participation in the women's association she says:

"I am a participant in the women's 'Sandoug' but my mother in-law is the one who gives them my share".

8.7 Questioning the loyalty of the in-laws towards the outsider

Safia's move to the Gezira for social reasons (marriage) induces her to move across different cultural contexts and stay among her respective ethnic group and places her under social isolation. She expressed this social isolation in terms of a feeling of loneliness that she experienced by facing an uncomfortable and threatening state imposed by her far kinfolks. She faced a troublesome personality in the family of her in-laws, the absence of a supportive person in addition to the biased position of her mother in-law. Her movement from her in-laws was mainly to avoid clashes and the influence of the in-laws. These incidences have driven her to understand the meaning of living away from her close kinfolk and to feel the bitterness of social isolation. Moreover, she was confronted with male authority in her respective ethnic group in which men play the role of mediators but, instead of judging who is guilty and who is innocent, they threaten and intimidate the women. However, Safia as the other women in the ethnic group conceive male authority as embedded in a traditional social system of gender order.

Social isolation is attributed to the unwillingness of the in-laws to accept the stranger as their son's wife and questioning their loyalty towards her. The women see the daughter in-law as a stranger, one of whose parents belongs to a different clan from that of one of the spouse's parents as well as being someone who was brought up outside the ethnic group. In addition, the women belonging to the same clan and consequently the same ethnic group see the woman as belonging to a different clan but the same ethnic group as an outsider. This implies that marriage within the same ethnic group is not sufficient to qualify women to be integrated in their respective ethnic group.

Safia's in-laws and other women of her respective ethnic group seem to avoid building social networks with her close kin. This attitude is considered questionable by Safia's close kin and embarrassing to her in front of them. Thus, her suffering resulting from her new receiving context is not only confined to her own lack of social support but extends to the lack of interest of her respective ethnic group in building social relations with her close kin. Hence, these incidences can be seen as causes of considerable social isolation among the members of same ethnic group/'cohesive subgroup'.

8.8 Living among respective ethnic group: an experience across different cultures

Safia is experiencing multiple forms of social and cultural changes in her sojourn among her respective ethnic group, which drive her to compare the way of life in her place of origin in terms of mutual social support and solidarity with her current experience among her respective ethnic group. She says, explaining her sufferings:

"I usually give birth by caesarean and my sister's daughter comes to stay with me for five months. After she leaves I suffer sometimes from stomach pain but I manage to do what I must do. I used to work a bit and have a rest and so on until I finish my housework. No one here helps me. This is their way of life. Unless one has her mother living in this village, no help is offered.... This is because I am a stranger to them. When I was with my relatives they would all help me, even when I was well; but I was forced to move with my husband. I have asked my husband several times if we could move to my relatives but he always refuses. The work makes me untidy and unable to look after myself."

When she realized the lack of interest of the women in engaging her in their social networks, she tried to find her way to narrow the social distance and to build some sort of social ties with them. She tried to transfer her own experiences in the area where she came from to these women. She says:

"The kind of relation between my relatives and the one between the people here is not the same... At the beginning, I tried to change the women of this village. I did tell them about my area and how people share life with each other, not only relatives, but also friends. They help each other, clean, cook and wash for each other, especially if one is sick. But here they still do not cooperate with me, except for my neighbours Nadia and Nagat - we help each other. When Nadia gave birth, Nagat and I used to cooperate to do the work for her. I used to fetch the water and clean the house. Nagat used to cook for her. We also used to work for her in the 'Khala' specially when her husband was still in Khartoum."

When Safia was asked about her knowledge of the women's associations in the camp and whether she is a participant she says:

"I am a member in the utensils association but the mother of Ali (mother in-law) is responsible for my participation and she is the one who pays my share to the women."

Social isolation is difficult to observe. However, it can be seen from a more microscopic vantage point in the interviews and appeared more clearly in a group discussion in which Noora and Safia were participants. The issue of caring for children by the in-laws or other women belonging to the same ethnic group came to the fore when Noora and Safia expressed themselves. Noora says:

"If I became sick my husband would do the work in the field and my neighbours Nagat and Nadia would help me at home. As for my daughter I always take her with me to the field because I have no one to look after her."

Safia agrees with Noora when she states:

"Since I moved to this place nobody has taken care of my children. I cannot remember anyone saying to me," "leave your daughters with me and I will look after them when you go to the field" or even offering help when I am sick. I always carry the small one on my back and the big one accompanies me."

Whilst the other women respondents in the focus group discussion assert their cooperative way of life and solidarity in terms of mutual social support and different forms of social obligations, with the exception of what she mentioned about caring of her daughters, Safia was just a listener. However, at the end when every woman had participated in the discussion I asked the group whether anyone had a comment or something to add, Safia exploded expressing her anger in talking about the kind of social relations which exist among the women in the camp and their relation with her. She consolidated her attack by bringing up some examples, such as how the women in the camp dealt with her when she moved to the camp and their way of welcoming her. It seemed that the other women were amazed while she was talking because none of them dared to say anything or interrupt her as they had previously throughout the discussion. As if correcting the other women, she said:

"I am telling you the truth honestly in front of these women. There are a lot of discriminations in the kind of relations in this village. When I lost some of my close relatives no one stood beside me. However, if one of them has lost someone they mourn with her and accompany her for condolences if she has to travel somewhere else but they do not even care to share the sorrow of the stranger who has moved from outside to stay among them. Their relationship is different; I mean that it is only between their relatives. I remember when I moved here and my relatives accompanied me, my cousin yelled[19] *upon our arrival, they were*

[19] Yelling of women is known in the African culture as an expression of joy and happiness. Thus, it is usually done in happy occasions.

looking at us over the 'Saraief'. Their nature is different and their manner differs from ours very much. If a stranger marries one of their men and comes to stay with them they deal with her in a way different from one of their own. Honestly they do not have any dealings with me but I deal with them in the same way that I was brought up. I am really affected with the way of life that I am experiencing with them. I hope that one day my husband will decide to return with me to my relatives because there are many differences between me and these people and this is what I do not like at all."

One of the women said to Safia angrily: *"Safia, bring your daughters from tomorrow and we will take care of them."*

At this moment most of the women started to talk at once. While I was trying to calm them in order not to lose control of the discussion, Noora, who agreed with Safia expressed herself loudly:

"All the people in this village are actually one tribe but if one was not born and has not been brought up among them, they do not consider this person one from them. On these bases, they deal with this person in a totally different way from the others who have been brought up among them." ".... They even discriminate between the locations of the houses. As you know, this village is a small one. How many houses are in this village? They are only 55 houses but they divided it into two. They call them the front quarter and the back quarter. Noora, Nagat, Nadia and I live in - the so called front quarter."

While one of the women tried to explain that this was not a matter of discrimination but just of naming the quarters, an unmarried woman interrupted, saying:

"Let me show you the issue. We also moved from Tchad and stayed for four years with our uncle in X-city (a city in the Gezira) *and after that we came here but we did not marry here. I mean that we do not marry one of our girls to someone here and neither do our sons marry from them. This is the issue."*

8.9 Social isolation in the 'cohesive subgroup'

In her sojourn among her respective ethnic group in the Gezira area, Safia experienced a lack of mutual social support and noticed the women's aversion to her. She could not change the women because they were able to repel the invasion of their social networks by an outsider. This means that the fact that she comes from outside and belongs to another clan will never be forgotten. Moreover, her mother in-law guides the supervision and control of her participation in the women's associations. This kind of behaviour shows that her mother in-law is acceptable to the women as a social reality which only serves to highlight her socially isolated position. However, in another line of argument, Safia as a social actor is able to take advantage of the social position of her mother in-law and her acceptability to the women of the respective ethnic group to guarantee her own membership in the women's associations. So, women such as Safia are more likely to experience social isolation among kinfolk of their spouses. They do not get social support from women of their respective ethnic group e.g. caring for their children or free engagement in the group social activities and *"seem to be at greatest risk of experiencing isolation"* (Adams et al. 1989: 728 - 29) from women belonging to the 'cohesive subgroup'. This social position drives Safia to compare the way of her life among her relatives to the one which she is experiencing in the new receiving context, a social reality which created a feeling of isolation in her and of being a stranger among the ethnic group to which she belongs. She is also confronted by: 1/ her husband's refusal to move with her in order to fulfil her aspirations of living among her close relatives and 2/ the reality that their (Safia and her spouse) work life is intertwined with the Gezira Scheme. In facing the reality of staying among her respective ethnic group, Safia as a social actor tried to transfer her experiences in social obligations of sharing and mutual social support to the women in the camp to narrow the social distance between her and them and consequently to resist and change her socially isolated position. In finding a way out of the trap of such social isolation, Safia and her two neighbours (Nadia and Nagat), who have a similar experience of the same social position of Safia in terms of being socially isolated, form a 'clique'. It is important to note here that Safia's two neighbours are Bargo who were also forced to move with their husbands and stay in the camp. One could therefore argue that it is evident that Safia is an actor in trying to escape the problem of having no extensive social networks with most of the women of her respective ethnic group. This is indicated by her desire for social support and the transferring of her experiences, which are met by the negative response of these women. Hence, unless she is an actor, the aversion of women to her as an outsider in addition to the attitude of her in-laws towards her may lead to extreme social isolation by discouraging her from engaging with her social network, something that in the past (i.e. among her close kin) was not a problem for her. In addition, unless Safia is an actor in her 'clique' she may lose the forms of mutual social support that her 'clique' members provide *"as a result of reduced contact with her social networks"* (La Veist 1997: 724).

8.10 Social isolation: an aggravating condition to attain livelihood

Research around the world confirms that migration is increasingly a livelihood strategy for rural and urban people (de Haan and Rogaly 2002). The concept of livelihood and its sustainability relates to; the living conditions of poor people, their opportunities and capabilities for well-being, their resilience, their necessary strategies for a means of living, their resource bases comprising of various assets and their ability to cope with and recover from stress and shock (Chambers and Conway 1992: 7 and Thieme 2006: 41). Relating social isolation to the concept of livelihood one could argue that social isolation is an aggravating condition on the women's attempts to attain well-being. Thus, social assimilation is one of the central components of livelihood. This is because isolation from the existing network (e.g. women belonging to the same ethnic group) deprives these women from taking advantage of the available 'social capital' such as the social ties and collective actions that women engaging in the network use as a resource for solving their problems, for mitigating their everyday life struggles and for benefiting from material and non-material resources. Such forms of exclusion may affect women's health "*The work makes me untidy and unable to look after myself*" and creates feelings of bitterness as a result of the isolation within the respective ethnic group. Social isolation also creates stress and a feeling of non-belonging and consequently causes a loss of interest in living among the respective ethnic group. This is evident from what Safia said: "*I am really affected by the way of life that I am experiencing with them. I hope that one day my husband will decide to return with me to my relatives because there are many differences between me and these people and this is what I do not like at all.*" Thus, these incidences affect the livelihood of the isolated women and consequently contradict both the concept of migration as a strategy for livelihood and the opinion that social networks provide a haven of support for migrants. To conclude, social assimilation into the social networks of respective ethnic group/'cohesive subgroup' is a new component to be added to the components of livelihood of the poor. However, as social actors, women realise a less isolating social position by forming their own 'clique'. Their choice to each other to form their own 'clique' and their reliability in this 'clique' explain that these women are 'knowledgeable' about their social isolated position and its aggravating effect on their well-being. Such social action explains that women are capable in developing strategies to overcome their problems in order to cope with life "*even under the most extreme forms of coercion.*" (Giddens 1984: 1 – 16; in Long 2001: 16). Thus, acquisition of such elements i.e. 'knowledgeability' and 'capability' explain that women are not only social actors in coping with life but they acquire agency as well.

8.11 Analysis of findings

Evidence shows that the Bargo women within each single 'cohesive subgroup' are characterized by social cohesion and have a rich organizational life in terms of organizing easily and collectively to achieve their goals either in the work sphere or in their private sphere. This specificity is embodied in their collectivity and reciprocal solidarity which are manifest in their collective actions and strategies, mutual collective work, social obligations of sharing and mutual social support. In spite of this distinctiveness, it is to be emphasized that social isolation is found as a social reality among the women belonging to this ethnic group.

Such social isolation can be attributed to different causes. Marriage outside the clan as well as the social reality of being brought up away from the ethnic group are social causations that place women under considerable social isolation among their respective ethnic group. This, on the one hand, means that the clan and the locality where women have been brought up matters and consequently brings into question the loyalty of the women belonging to the same ethnic group towards the isolated women. On the other hand, the difference between the social and cultural context in which (the isolated) women have been brought up and the one of their respective ethnic group plays an important role. The drastic difference between the localities and loss of the advantages of the former locality (where the women were brought up) create a social distance between women belonging to the same ethnic group as well as fear among women of not fulfilling their goals in the new receiving context, thus deepening the feeling of social isolation among them. These factors, in addition to the traditional rural hard work in the field, create a feeling of non-belonging whilst living among the respective ethnic group and consequently a dream of a return to the former locality in order to achieve specific goals.

Excluding women within their respective ethnic group from taking advantage of the 'social capital' available to the women engaging in the network creates social isolation. One could argue that such social isolation is an aggravating condition on the women's attempts to attain their own well-being. Thus, the correlation that necessitates a consideration of social assimilation as one of the components of livelihood is a new contribution to the social networks theory and analysis, proposed by this study. It has also been demonstrated, however, that such social isolation can bind the isolated women together.

As social actors they found their way to a less isolating social position by forming their own 'clique'. In spit of the fact that the isolated women have no extensive social networks outside their own 'clique', by engaging within this 'clique' they could avoid 'extreme social isolation'. In addition socially isolated women as social actors could manage to take advantage of the social position of other women engaging in the network, as it is evident in the case of Safia, to guarantee their membership in the women's associations. Furthermore, the traditional male authority and the social and gender order structured the (undeniable) social isolation of women within the community of their respective ethnic origin. Although women migrants accepted male authority and the gender order as a form of tradition, by applying their own strategies women as social actors could escape the traditional male authority in order to fulfil their own interest.

9. Conclusion

Examining the social networks of women migrants engaged in the agricultural labour force of the Gezira Scheme, a combination of theoretical approaches guided the analysis with the objective of broadening and strengthening it. Different theoretical notions of social network analysis and applications that motivate the analysis and interpretation of the empirical data, such as 'transitivity', 'clique', 'cohesive subgroup', 'reciprocity' and 'social capital' are used. The analysis is also based on an actor-oriented approach developed by Norman Long (1992, 2001). The theoretical and methodological perspectives of an actor-oriented approach offers valuable insights into processes of 'social construction', as well as the 'heterogeneity' in analysing the social networks of women migrants in the Gezira Scheme. The advantage of the actor-oriented approach specially suits the analysis of these social networks through which social forms, social processes and arrangements emerge and are consolidated in the everyday lives (Long 2001: 49) of these women with more or less similar social and economic conditions.

The theory of agency as an important requirement of an actor-oriented perspective is crucial in examining women migrants' strategies in their work sphere as well as in their private sphere. The concept of agency is found to be useful for example, in analysing the way women as social actors concentrate on their social networks as important means by which they construct collective actions to solve the problems arising within the work sphere and in their private sphere. Agency is an important theoretical concept in analysing how the women migrants process their lifeworlds, learn from the experiences of others and act upon them, for example in the case of traditional social practices. Furthermore, the theoretical importance of agency is that it is a concept through which women as social actors use the circumstances available to them by means of generation and manipulation of their social networks and by their decision-making processes in the work sphere. The particular elements of agency used are the 'knowledgeability' and 'capability' of women as means of resolving their problems of their everyday life.

Examining the social networks of women migrants in the Gezira Scheme by drawing upon a sociological approach provides new important insights into the social networks theory and proposes new contributions to the social network theory and analysis. It also postulates additions in several places to support Long's actor-oriented perspective. However, the contribution of the study is not just as an addition to the postulates of Norman Long. To be more precise, this study proposes that it is not satisfactory to study only how 'heterogeneity' in terms of diverse social forms is generated, as Long postulates, but that such an approach must also demonstrate an understanding of why these differences are produced – a new contribution by this study. To this end, the analysis tackles the question of differential responses; in terms of the differences in the women's social processes, social practices and social organizations. It confronts why, for instance, some ethnic groups practice more solidarity and close social interactions than others or, in other words, why some are more differentiated and diversified than others.

Women's social networks serve multiple purposes and facilitate a wide range of settings. The key insights of women's social networks are that the available means and contacts through which women acquire information about work and find work opportunities vary. These variations indicate the existence of 'heterogeneity' in the way women migrants construct their social networks to achieve their goals as female labour. 'Heterogeneity', which is remarkable in the structure of diverse social relations including gender relations, shapes processes of information diffusion and women's work negotiations where there appear to be considerable differences in these processes. These differences, evident within the same ethnic group as well as between different ethnic groups, are attributable to the dissimilarity in the ways women construct their social networks within the existing ethnic diversity of the migrants and to the cultural discourse available to each of these ethnic groups.

The 'social heterogeneity' that distinguishes the women migrants' social reality is also evident in the different strategies constructed by different ethnic groups and the dissimilarity in the means of social organisation between 'cohesive subgroups' and even within a single 'cohesive subgroup'. 'Heterogeneity' of women migrants' social forms is a common feature of their social reality, despite the commonalities of the properties that distinguish the migrants' 'cohesive subgroups' and the similarity of the circumstances in which they live and perform their labour in the Gezira Scheme. Hence, this provides evidence of the actor-oriented approach which embraces different responses in similar structural circumstances, even if the conditions appear to be relatively homogeneous, a feature that reflects the meaning of 'social heterogeneity' (Long 2001:11 and 21). In addition, this study proves that social networks in rural settings are heterogeneous, a social reality considered a new contribution to the social networks theory – one not recognised by several social networks analysts, who instead consider social networks in rural settings to be homogeneous.

The homogeneity that this study recognises is explicated in the properties of the 'cohesive subgroups'. The theoretical importance of 'cohesive subgroups' lies in the social forces that operate through relative cohesion within the subgroup. These social forces aid women in using 'transitivity logic' to connect with the male tenants where there are either direct or no contacts between the two groups. Using these ideas, the general properties of the migrants' 'cohesive subgroups' that influence the formalisation of the women's social networks are; ethnocentricity, the social discourse associated with the ethnic identity, the sharing of existential space resulting in closeness and 'reachability', intimacy and belonging, as well as group identity, evinced by the engagement in similar forms of labour and the sharing of a spirit of common destiny. These commonalities, which explain how the women's relations within a single 'cohesive group' are associated, are decisive resources for ensuring work opportunities for women as one of the primary benefits of women's social networks.

The significance of weak ties is proven in the context of the Gezira Scheme through the existence of transitive relations. It is evident that the application of 'transitivity logic' does not only permit the analysis of relationships within a single 'cohesive subgroup' but also of inter-groups' relationships as well as those of gender relations. Therefore, 'transitivity' has been shown to be a key property in women's social networks as well as a common feature explaining women migrants' social structure. This is evident particularly in the way women get access to information about work and find work opportunities. Thus, transitivity is considered as a leading force in the organisation of heterogeneous social groups. It is an important resource in enabling women to enter the work sphere, providing for a higher level of women's mobility within such a sphere and also playing a significant role in affecting social cohesion.

The reason that 'transitivity' is a compelling force in women's social networks can be attributed to the fact that the structures of the communities (the migrants and the local community) living in the Gezira Scheme are so diverse. The lodging of the migrants in groups based on ethnicity indicates why several ethnic groups and cultural discourses form these groups as clusters. The forms of transitive relations in terms of dissimilarity in the social positions that the women migrants occupy in the work negotiations are grounded on their ethnic background. The availability of cultural discourses of heterogeneous ethnic groups of the migrants living in the Gezira Scheme is manifest where the work negotiations are governed by gender. Thus, women migrants' work negotiations are governed by their gender and the ethnic difference between them and the men tenants. On these grounds, ethnicity, gender and clusterability lead to a consideration of the concept of transitivity. In view of these facts, application of the 'transitivity logic' has, therefore, become a necessity in the social context of the Gezira Scheme. Thus, 'transitivity' is not only associated with 'clusterability' as such, as it is found in the social networks theory, but also in the consideration of the concepts of ethnicity and gender - a new contribution to social networks theory and analysis by this study.

Reliance of the women migrants on their co-ethnic men to be their intermediary contacts with the men outside their ethnic groups signifies that ethnic identity is consciously and keenly felt by women. However, belonging to the same ethnic group as the women is not the only decisive factor in qualifying the men migrants as intermediaries for these women. It is the women themselves who assign whom among the men of the same ethnic group they trust and in whom they have confidence to be their intermediary contacts. Furthermore, as a result of such a choice the men concerned acquire prestige and power compared to the other men in their respective 'ethnic group'. In this view, women's social networks are a source of male power. On these grounds, trust, confidence, power and prestige are important concepts in the analysis of gender relations as a new dimension in social networks theory. Another link to this contribution is that social networks in the work sphere are more than a means of circulating information and providing work opportunities. Social networks serve to challenge or reinforce cultural forms of organisations, particularly gender and gender relations. Gender relations as a form of social relations embedded in the cultural constitution of the migrant communities shape the structure of contacts and the kinds of ties within the women's social networks, not only between women and men but also between women. This evidence brings about new cultural expectations about gender and demonstrates how gender and social networks as isolated fields might communicate with one another.

Although women migrants' engagement in the work sphere in the Gezira Scheme has not altered the gender ideologies altogether, women migrants were able to make use of the 'transitivity logic'. This is made plausible either through taking advantage of the wide social horizons of men migrants or through manipulating their social networks with women outside the migrant communities, or through taking advantage of women migrants who are adjacent actors to the men tenants. Unlike the trauma associated with many cases where women are considered as subordinated, suppressed or excluded, this study comes out with a new understanding of women's social position and social networking. It provides evidence that women are not passive recipients but, conversely, social actors in their societies. This is manifest where women benefit from finding work opportunities not restricted to increasing the household income, as has been reported by many scholars, but goes beyond that into broader achievements. Such achievements can be cited as economic networks, mobility and a number of others associated with the acquirement of agency. Hence, these achievements resulted in increased social power and decision-making. In addition to that, women influence the tenants' activities to realise more work opportunities. This action can be interpreted as a strategy by which women exercise some kind of 'power' through using their rights to demonstrate their 'negotiation power' when they need it in order to process their lifeworlds. I therefore argue that women acquire agency and are social actors, evident in the way women benefit from the construction of their social networks and their ability to take advantage of the given circumstances, a significant finding considered by this study as an addition to Long's actor-oriented approach.

To weave the threads together, construction of women migrants' social networks is not confined to the frontiers of the migrants' social setting but expanded to reach other communities. By means of formalisation and manipulation of their social networks women migrants have shown themselves to be able to intertwine their social networks with the other existing social groups in the Gezira Scheme, a social reality that shows that migration is not an individualistic process and is a fertile ground for the construction of social networks. In addition, the way women migrants as social actors shape their everyday life by means of their social networks makes migration less risky for them.

Women as social actors jointly construct strategies by means of their social networks in terms of collective actions to solve problems arising within the work sphere. Women carry out mutual collective group work, e.g. *'Nafeer'* for serving food as an alternative to payment, in order to solve the problem of scarce financial resources that hinder the migrants' ability to pay wages for hired labour. Such forms of collective work in which reciprocity and exchange relations are embedded necessitate the existence of social obligations, loyalty and trust among the key actors. These properties are made available to the migrants' 'cohesive subgroups' since they are small groups in which each person knows all other members of the subgroup. Such properties, in addition to the others of the 'cohesive subgroup', provide for linkages between its members, proving that 'cohesive subgroups' and the women's 'cliques' acquire 'social capital'. This is considered an important resource in the construction of collective actions since the members of the collective groups should forgo self-interest and act in the interests of the collectivity. In carrying out a collective harvest women show commitment, common understanding and principles emanating from the existence of a dense network of ties binding the members of a single 'cohesive subgroup' and from the ability of women to utilise these ties effectively.

The analysis not only depicts the strategies or collective actions of women and how such strategies and social forms are different but also develops the analysis further by interpreting why women belonging to some ethnic groups have rich organizational life in terms of the ability to organize for common goals quite easily, while others have a poor organizational life and seem to be unable to mobilize resources. In spite of the existence of generalized reciprocity and social solidarity that mould the outlook of the women migrants these differences have been found as a social reality. This specificity, embodied in the characteristics of the group, has been found to be linked to historical background, social events, variations in culture and social change. Despite the fact that specific ethnic groups have a rich organisational life in terms of collectivity, mutual social support and reciprocal social solidarity, the social reality shows that social isolation does exist among these groups. By structuring the pool from which network members are drawn, differences in clan, locality in which the women have been brought up and the social relationships in which these women are embedded contribute to the distinctiveness of women belonging to one ethnic group and is consequently a cause of considerable social isolation for women living within their respective ethnic group. This form of social isolation excludes these women from taking advantage of the available 'social capital' which women engaging in the network use as a resource for solving their problems and mitigating their everyday life struggles. Such social isolation creates a feeling of non-belonging to the respective ethnic group, a feeling of being out of place and of stress. These feelings and lack of social support consequently cause a loss of interest in those living among this group. Thus, this social position negatively affects the opportunities for the well-being of the isolated women. In other words, social isolation is an aggravating condition on the women's attempts to attain well-being. Therefore, the correlation that necessitates consideration of the social assimilation (a reverse of social isolation) as one of the components of livelihoods is considered a new contribution by this study to the social networks theory and analysis.

Construction of 'traditional social security' represents a cornerstone in the cultural constitution of the women migrants. Women migrants encounter various problems in their private sphere which induce them to construct collective actions and strategies for security. They live in a disadvantageous economic and social position in which they have no access to 'formal social security'. What is, however, most striking is that these constraints induce women to realize the significance of their own social networks by means of which they develop a collective identity and common forms of organisation in the institutionalisation of their own 'neo-informal' social associations for securing their livelihoods. Hence, new dimensions of actors' strategies emerged in the work sphere of the receiving social context by means of social networks of the women migrants and, consequently, they achieve their common goals a social reality which shows that women acquire 'effective agency'. A striking example is that this collectivity is evident in the way women take advantage of their wage labour in terms of investment of the return received from their collective wage work in establishing their collective savings boxes and keeping them functioning. Thus, the emergence of new savings systems of the women migrants with the objective of supporting the poor ones is considered a new strategy for security in the social context of the Gezira Scheme. One could here argue that examining women migrants' social security could help rural sociologists to understand the mechanisms which underline many of the economic and social challenges facing rural women.

By means of their collective actions, strategies, mutual social support and social obligations of sharing that form a foundation of women migrants' 'social security', women are found to be bound by several social ties. In reality, women's activities for security are embedded in the different kinds of relationships between the different social actors involved. Thus, different women's networks include inter-household relations and women's 'cliques', traditional relations e.g.

neighbourhood relations, ethnic relations, kin relations, social action groups or peer groups.

Joint activities are evidence of what is often referred to as the 'overlapping' of women's activities with their social relations. It is also evident that the forms of 'social capital' available to the women migrants are key elements in the fulfilment of their 'social security'. Women's construction of their 'social security' indicates the material as well as non-material significance of their social networks. Furthermore, this social system that women migrants have generated has maintained solidarity and 'reciprocity' not only among women belonging to the same ethnic group but also between women of heterogeneous ethnic identities. Hence, social networks among women migrants are decisive in the fulfilment of their 'social security'. This signifies that women's social networks constitute their chief resources (White 1992: 88) and centres of power.

References

Adam, Mohamed A. 1996, The Policy Impacts on Farmers' Production and Resource Use in the Irrigated Scheme of Gezira, Sudan: A Case of Change from A Controlled Subsidized System to A Free Market Mode of Production, Köln Wissenschaftsverlag Vauk, Germany.

Adams, James P.; Kaufman Allan V.; and Dressler, William W. 1989, "Predictors of Social Isolation in older southern adults: A cross-racial Analysis", Journal of Applied Gerontology, 8, Pp. 365-381.

Baasher, Mustafa M. 1987, "The Structure of Agricultural Production and the Role of Women in Different Farming Systems in Central and Eastern Sudan (With an Emphasis on Commercial Large Scale Agriculture)", In: FAO and the Khartoum Polytechnic, College of Agricultural Studies. Interim Report, National Conference on the Role of Women in Agricultural and Rural Development in the Sudan. Rome: FAO.

Barnett, Tony and Abdelkarim, Abbass 1991, Sudan: the Gezira Scheme and Agricultural Transition, School of Development Studies, University of East Anglia, Frank Cass & Co., London.

Barnett, Tony 1977, The Gezira Scheme: An Illusion of Development, London, Frank Cass.

Bernard Russell, Harvey 2000, Social Research Methods: Qualitative and Quantitative Approaches, Sage Publications.

Bernstein, Henry; Johnson, Hasel and Thomas, Alan 1992, "Labor Regimes and Social Change under Colonialism" in: Allen, Tim (eds.), Poverty and Development in the 1990's, Oxford University Press.

Blalock Jr., Hubert M. 1991, "Understanding Social Inequality: Modeling Allocation Processes" in: Social Theory: Books from SAGE, SAGE Library in Social Research, London, Pp. 11.

Boddy, Janice 1989, Wombs and Alien Spirits, Madison: University of Wisconsin Press.

Bryceson, Deborah 2000, "Policy Responses: Sustainable Rural Livelihoods and Social Capital Approaches", in: Natural Resource Perspectives, Number 52, April 2000, http://www.odi.org.uk/nrp/52.html.

Buchenrieder, Gertrud and Dufhues, Thomas 2006, "Open Issues and Implications for Measuring Individual Social Capital in Developing Countries" in: Buchenrieder, Gertrud and Dufhues Thomas (eds) Making Rural Households' Livelihoods More Resilient: The Importance of Social Capital and Underlying Social networks, 26th International Conference of Agricultural Economists (IAAE), Leibnitz Institute of Agricultural Development in Central Europe (IAMO), Germany, Pp. 24 - 42

Buchenrieder, Gertrud 2006, "Issues and Evidence of Social Networks in Boosting Rural Households' Welfare" in: Buchenrieder, Gertrud and Dufhues Thomas (eds) Making Rural Households' Livelihoods More Resilient: The Importance of Social Capital and Underlying Social Networks, 26th International conference of Agricultural Economists (IAAE), Leibnitz Institute of Agricultural Development in Central Europe (IAMO), Germany, Pp.3 – 23.

Burt, Ronald S. and Minor, Michael J. 1983, Applied Network Analysis, California, Sage Publications.

Chambers, Robert and Conway, Gordon R. February 1992, "Sustainable Rural Livelihoods: Practical Concepts for the 21st Century", Discussion Paper, IDS Discussion Paper No. 296, Institute of Development Studies (IDS), University of Sussex, Brighton, England.

Coleman James S. 1988 "Social Capital in the Creation of Human Capital" in: American Journal of sociology Volume 94 Supplement, University of Chicago, S95-S120.

Culwick, G. M. 1955, The Human Factor in the Gezira Scheme: A report, Sudan Gezira Board, Sudan.

··· 1955, Interim Report on Social Research in the Gezira, The Sudan Gezira Board (SGB), Barakat, Sudan, Pp 1 – 59.

Dannecker, Petra 1999, "Conformity or Resistance? Women Workers in the Garment Factories in Bangladesh", Working Paper No. 326, Sociology of Development Research Centre, University of Bielefeld, Germany.

De Haan, Arjan and Rogaly, Ben 2002, "Special Issues on Labour Mobility and Rural Society", The Journal of Development Studies, Frank Cass & Co. Ltd., London.

De Haan, Leo and Zoomers, Annelies 2002, Exploring the Frontiers of Livelihoods Research in: Development and change 36(1), Pp. 27-47.

De Soto, Hermine H. and Panzig Christel 1995, "Women, gender and Rural Development, East Germany Before and after Unification" in: Altmann, Uta und Tehereni-Krönner, Parto, Frauen in der Länlichen Entwicklung, Volume 1, Landwirtschaftlich-Gärtenrische Fakultät Berlin.

Dey, Ian 1993, Qualitative Data analysis: A User-Friendly Guide for Social Scientists, London and New York: Routledge.

Elkarib, Aisha. K. et.al. 1996, "Women Development in Agriculture", Agricultural Conference, Ministry of Agriculture, Ministry of Irrigation, Ministers Council's Head Quarters, Khartoum, Sudan (Arabic version).

Giddens, Anthony 1984, The Construction of Society: Online of a Theory of Structuration, Cambridge: Polity Press.

Gittel, Ross and Vidal Avis 1998, Community Organising: Building Social Capital as a Development Strategy, Newsbury Park, CA, USA, Sage Publications.

Granovetter, Mark 1973, "The Strength of Weak Ties" in: American Journal of Sociology Vol. 78, No. 6, Pp. 1360 – 1380.

··· 1974, Getting a Job: A Study of Contacts and Careers, Cambridge: Harvard University Press.

··· 1985, "Economic Action and Social Structure: The Problem of Embeddedness", in: American Journal of Sociology, Volume 91 Number 3, Pp. 481-510.

Grätz, Tilo 2000, "Gold Trade in the Atakora Region (Republic of Benin): Social Networks beyond the State", Halle/Saale, A paper presented in Africa Conference, 2000, Leipzig, Germany.

GRPMU and IDCA Summary Report, 1994, "Migratory Labour Settlements", Gezira Rehabilitation Project Monitoring Unit (GRPMU) and The Irish Development Co-operation Agency IDCA, Planning and Socio-Economic Research Unit, Sudan Gezira Board (SGB), Sudan.

Hagar, Igbal M. A. 1992, The Role of Women in Agriculture in the Gezira Scheme, Planning and Scio-economic Unit, The Sudan Gezira Board, Sudan.

Hagar, Igbal M. A. 1996, Women Migrants to Gezira for Cotton picking: Contributions and Problems, The Seventh Gender Research Competition of: Organization for Social Science Research in Eastern Africa (OSSREA), The Sudan Gezira Board, Sudan.

Hashim, Muhammad Jalal Ahmed 2004, To Be or Not to Be: Sudan At Crossroads, Beacon House, Stokenchurch, Bucks, England.

http://www.consecol.org/vol5/iss2/art13/.

http://www.Essybank.co.uk.

Isikdag, Fatma 1991, Household livelihood strategies and women's agricultural work: the Gezira Scheme, Sudan, Thesis (Ph. D. in Economics), University of California, Berkeley, published by University Microfilms International (UMI) Dissertation Information Service, USA

Kabeer, Naila (November) 1992, Triple Role, Gender Roles, Social Relations: The political Sub-Text of Gender Training, Discussion Paper 313, Institute of Development Studies, University of Sussex, England.

Kaleta Andrzej et. al. 2001, Revitalization of Rural areas in Europe, Vol. IV, Rural and Agricultural Transformation in Central Europe, Institute of Sociology, Nicolaus Copernicus University in Torun, Poland.

Kasarjyan, Milada and Kroff, Rüdiger 2006, "Improving the Functioning of Armenian Rural Financial Markets: A Social Capital perspective" in: Buchenrieder, Gertrud and Dufhues Thomas(eds) Making Rural Households' Livelihoods More Resilient: The Importance of Social Capital and Underlying Social Networks, 26th International conference of Agricultural Economists (IAAE), Leibnitz Institute of Agricultural Development in Central Europe (IAMO), Germany, Pp. 71-85.

Kertzer, David I. and Madison, Oker B. B. 1981, "Women's Age-Set Systems in Africa: The Latuka of Southern Sudan", Chapter 6, in: Dimensions: Aging,Culture, and Health. CL Fry, (ed.), Pp. 109-130.

Krishna, Anirudh and Uphoff Norman 2002, "Social Capital and Water Shed Management" In: The Role of Social Capital in development: An Empirical Assessment, Grootaert, C. and Th. Van Bastelaer (eds.), Cambridge, UK, University Press, Pp. 85-124.

Kwiecinska, Monika 2001, "Local Communities" Pp. 115-127 in: Kaleta, Andrzej et. al. 2001, Revitalization of Rural areas in Europe, Vol. IV, Rural and Agricultural Transformation in Central Europe, Institute of Sociology, Nicolaus Copernicus University in Torun, Poland.

La Veist, Thomas et. al. 1997, "Extreme Social isolation, Use of community-Based Senior Support Services, and Mortality Among African American Elderly Women", American Journal of Community Psychology, Vol. 25, No. 5, 1997.

Lachenmann, Gudrun 1998, "Construction of Social Security, Modernity, and Tradition in West Africa." Working Paper No. 304, Sociology of Development Research Centre, University of Bielefeld, Germany.

··· 1997, "Informal Social Security in Africa from a Gender perspective", in: Searching for Security: Women's Responses to Economic Transformations, Isa Baud and Ines Smyth (eds.), London: Routledge, Pp. 45-66.

Long, Norman 1992, Battlefields of Knowledge: The Interlocking of Theory and Practice in Social Research and Development, Norman Long and Ann Long (eds.), London: Routledge.

··· 1992, "From Paradigm Lost to Paradigm Regained: The case of An Actor-oriented Sociology of Development", in: Battlefields of Knowledge, The Interlocking of Theory and Practice in Social Research and Development, Norman Long and Ann Long (eds.), London: Routledge, Pp. 16-46.

··· 2001, Development Sociology: Actor perspectives. London: Routledge.

··· 2002, "An Actor-oriented Approach to Development Intervention", Background paper prepared for APO Meeting (in Tokyo 22-26 April 2002), Wageningen University, The Netherlands.

Macharia, Kinuthia 1988, "Social Networks: Ethnicity and the Informal Sector in Nairobi", IDS/WP-Working Paper No. 463, Institute for Development Studies, University of Nairobi, Kenya.

McCallister, Lynne and Fischer, Claude S. 1983, "Procedure for Surveying Personal Networks", Chapter 3, in: Burt, Ronald S. and Minor, Michael J. (eds.). Applied Network Analysis, California, Pp. 75-88.

Meier, Barbara and Knörr, Jacqueline (eds.) 2000, Women and Migration: Anthropological Perspective, Campus Verlag. Frankfurt/New York and St. Martin's Press. New York.

Menjivar, Cecilia 1995, "Kinship Networks Among immigrants: lessons From a Qualitative Comparative Approach", in: International Journal of Comparative Sociology, Vol. XXXVI – Numbers 3-4 December 1995, E.J. Brill (Editor), Leiden, Pp. 219-232.

Moghadam, Valentine M. 2005, Globalizing Women: Transnational Feminist Networks, The Johns Hopkins University Press, Baltimore and London.

Nageeb, Salma Ahmed 2004, New Spaces and Old Frontiers: Women, Social Space, and Islamization in Sudan, USA: LEXINGTON Books.

O'Brien, Jay 1980, Agricultural Labour and Development in Sudan, University of Connecticut.

Padmanabhan, Martina Aruna 2002, Trying to Grow - Gender Relations and Agricultural Innovations in Northern Ghana, Münster: LIT VERLAG.

Pieterse, Jan Nederveen 2000, "Social Capital, Migration and Cultural Difference: Beyond Ethnic Economics", Working Paper Series No. 327, Institute of Social Studies (ISS), The Hague.

Platte, Editha 2000, "Pioneers in the Lake: Female Migrants in the Lake Chad Region of North-eastern Nigeria", in Women and Migration: Anthropological Perspective, edited by Jacqueline Knörr and Barbara Meier, Campus Verlag. Frankfurt/New York and St. Martin's Press. New York, Pp. 197-211.

Powel, Walter W. and Smith-Doerr, Laurel 1994, "Networks and Economic Life", Chapter 15, in: Smelser, Neil J.; Swedberg, Richard (eds.), The Hand Book of Economic Sociology, New York, Russell SAGE Foundation, Pp. 368 - 402.

Portes, A. 1998, Social Capital: Its Origins and Applications in Modern Sociology, Annual Review of Sociology, 24, Pp. 1-24.

Purewel, Tej 1998, "Structural Adjustment and its Impacts on Women", A paper presented in a public lecture in AUW in Omdurman, Sudan, 1998, Manchester University, England.

Radcliffe, Sarah A. 1986, "Gender Relations, Peasant Livelihood, Strategies and Migration": a Case Study from Cuzco, Peru, in: Bull, Latin Am. Res., Vol. 5, No. 29 – 47,Printed in Great Britain.

Rogers, Everett M. 1981, Communication Networks, The Free Press: A Division of Macmillan Publishing Co., New York.

Santen, Jose van and Schaafsma, Juliette 2000, "Mafa Women and Migration", in: Women and Migration: Anthropological Perspective, edited by Jacqueline Knörr and Barbara Meier, 2000, Campus Verlag. Frankfurt/New York and St. Martin's Press. New York, Pp. 21-61.

Schmidt, Heike 2000, Gender and Power – Changing Political Institutions in Pre-colonial Africa, A Paper Presented in Africa Conference, Leipzig, Germany.

Schultz, Ulrike 2005, Geschlecht, Macht, Familie-Localisierung und Aushandlung von "Moderne" in sudanesischen Haushalten und Familien, Habilitationschrift, Politik- und Sozialwissenschaften, Freien Universität - Berlin, Deutschland.

Schott, Rüdiger, 1988, "Traditional Systems of Social Security in Africa and their Present Day Crisis in West Africa", in: Benda-Beckmann et al. (eds.), Between Kinship and The State: Social Security and the Law in Developing Countries, Pp. 89-108.

Scott, John 1991, Social Network Analysis: Sage, London.

Shaaeldin, Elfatih (ed.) 1987, The Evolution of Agrarian Relations in the Sudan: A Reader, The Hague.

Smelser, Neil J. and Swedberg, Richard (eds.) 1994, The Hand Book of Economic Sociology, New York, Russell SAGE Foundation.

Spring, Anita 2001, "Beyond a Rural Subsistence: Positive Effects of Agricultural Commercialisation on Women Farmers: A New Paradigm", Chapter 2 in: Webb, Patrick; Weinberger, Katinka (eds.) 2001, Women Farmers: Enhancing Rights, Recognition and Productivity, The Centre for Development Research, Bonn.

Straus, Anselm L. and Corbin, Juliet 1990, Basics of Qualitative research: Grounded Theory Procedures and Techniques, London: Sage.

Streiffeler, Friedhelm and Piszczek, Elwira 2004, "The Situation of Illegal Polish Seasonal Workers in the German Agriculture", Presented at Institute of Sociology, Nicolaus Copernicus University in Torun, Poland.

Thieme, Susan 2006, Social Networks and Migration: Far West Nepalese labour Migrants in Delhi, Münster: LIT VERLAG.

Wasserman, Stanley and Faust, Katherine 1994, Social Network Analysis: Methods and Applications, USA, Cambridge University Press.

Watts, D. J. 2003, Six degrees. The science of a connected age, London, UK: The Random House Group Ltd.

Wellman, Barry 1992, "Which Types of Ties and Networks Provide What Kinds of Social Support?" In: "Advances in Group Processes", Vol. 9, 1992 by JAI Press, Pp. 207-235.

White, Sarah C. 1992, Arguing with the Crocodile: Gender and Class in Bangladesh, London, Zed Books.

··· 1992, "Arguing with the Crocodile: Gender, Class in Bangladesh", London Zed. Books, 186pp in: Smith 1994 in: Official Journal of Rural Sociological Society, Vol. 59, Published in Montana State University, Bozeman, Pp.557 – 558.

Woolcock, Michael 2001, "The Place of Social Capital in Understanding Social and Economic Outcomes", Isuma, Canadian Journal of Policy Research, 2(1), Pp. 11 - 17.

··· 2003, "Social Capital" in: Christensen, K. and Levinson, D. (eds.), Encyclopedia of community: From the Village to the Virtual World, Sage, Pp. 1258-1262.

World Bank Report No. 20398-SU, (Oct. 27) 2000, Sudan Options for Sustainable development of the Gezira Scheme, Prepared Jointly by the Government of the Sudan and Macroeconomics 2, Country Department 6 – Eritrea, Ethiopia, Somalia, Sudan – Africa Region, Washington.

www.birf.info/home/bi-tools/qlinks_s.html. Definition im Kontext; Definitionen von social isolation in Web.

Yousif, Galal Mahmoud 1997, The Gezira Scheme: The Greatest on Earth under One Management, Africa University House for Printing, Khartoum, Sudan.

Yousif, Hassan Musa 1992, Intensity and Consequences of Migration and Immigration on Women in Agricultural Development, Sudan.

Zhu Ling and Jiang Zhongyi 2001, Chapter 13, "Gender Inequality in the Land Tenure System of China" in: Webb, Patrick; Weinberger, Katinka (eds.) 2001, Women Farmers: Enhancing Rights, Recognition and Productivity, The Centre for Development Research, Bonn.

Appendix 1: List of abbreviations

AUW	Ahfad University for Women
DSRC	Development Studies and Research Center
GRPMU	Gezira Rehabilitation Project Monitoring Unit
GS	Gezira Scheme
IAS	Individual Account System
IDCA	The Irish Development Co-operation Agency
ISS	Institute of Social Studies
IWGDS	Institute of Women, Gender and Development Studies
JAS	Joint Account System
SGB	Sudan Gezira Board
THL	Tenants' household labour
U of K	University of Khartoum
WB	World Bank

Appendix 2: Glossary of local expressions

Abraih	A special drink of 'Ramadan'
Arab	An ethnic term used for the people from the Northern part of the Sudan. The migrants call the people of the local community as Arab. (When it is used from here after it indicates people of the local community). (For more details about the use of this term refer to note No. 1 in chapter 5)
Bargo	An ethnic group from Tchad
Beni Halba	An ethnic group from Tchad
Camboo	Camp
Daim	A huge camp which is occupied by various ethnic groups
Dangada	Land sub-leasing
Eldangada	The land sub-leasing
Eid	A religious festival of Muslims e.g. Ramadan's fest. Ayad is a plural of Eid
Elcamboo	The camp
Eltouriah	The hoe
Fanoos	Kerosene lamp
Goffa	A basket. It is used in the Gezira as a measure in cotton picking
Hawasha	A tenancy
Hawashat	Plural of a tenancy (tenancies)

Karamah A meal, which is made especially in some social occasions. Bargo call the meal, which is prepared as a closure of a mourning occasion *'Karamah'*

Iddah House utensils

Eliddah The house utensils

Kardafa This is a well-known name among the migrants, at least in Wad Ellaithie, used for the people who migrated from Kordofan. Kordofan is a region in the West of Sudan.

Kargaka A big water pipe which is used by villagers or camp settlers for pumping water

Khala Is an Arabic word means an open area. The people of the Sudan and the migrants use it locally for the agricultural field/(s)

Khalwa An informal preschool religious education in which the Koran & religious issues are being taught

Khartoum The capital of Sudan

Kissra Local bread of the Sudan, which is made of Sorghum and is considered as a stable food of the rural people

Mecca A city in Saudia Arabia and one of the important places which pilgrims visit

Midangidah A woman who works as a land subleaser

Mimawia A woman who belongs to Mima. Mima is one of the clans of the Bargo ethnic group

Musaada An Arabic word means help

Nafeer A form of mutual collective work

Jadawil	Is a plural of Jadwal, which means a small water canal
Sandoug	A traditional savings box
Sanadeeg	Is a plural of *'Sandoug'*
Sareef	A house fence made of straw and wood
Saraief	Is a plural of Sareef
Schoolboys	It is used for school children i.e. girls and boys
Selaihab	Is a clan of the Bargo ethnic group
Sharia	Islamic laws
Sheikh	The camp or village leader
Ramadan	The fasting month of Muslims
Tama	An ethnic group from Tchad
Zagawa	An ethnic group from Darfur region in the West of Sudan, rooted in Tchad
Zakat	Islamic taxes, which is collected from the prosperous people and should be given to the poor.

Appendix 3: Research locality No. 1

Appendix 4: Research locality No. 2

Daim Wad Ellaithie

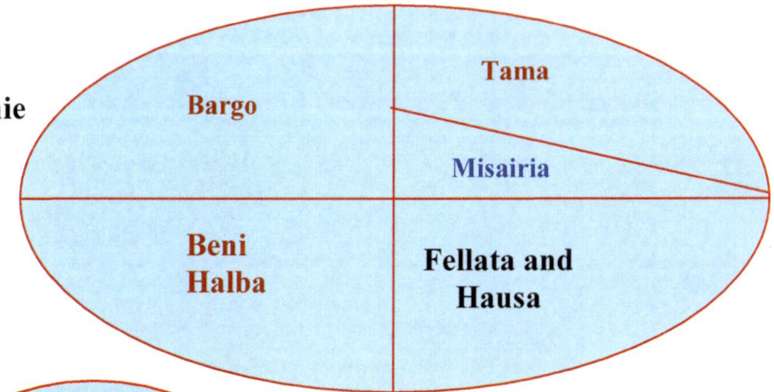

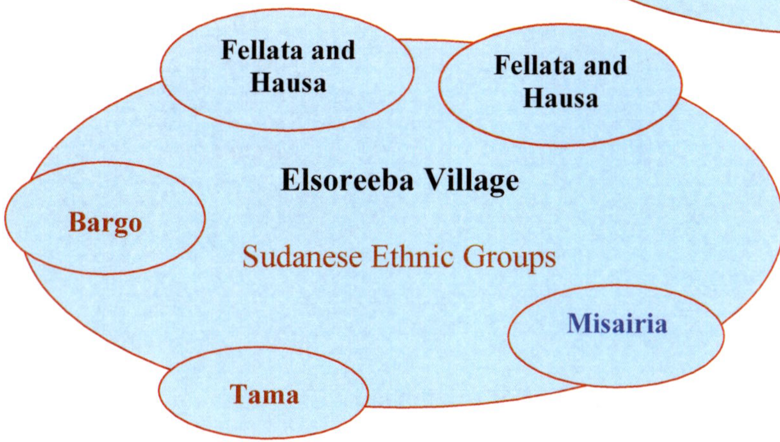